Eve Parsons

# Roscroggan

Wartime hardship and family strife
in an idyllic Cornish village

Eve Parsons

# Roscroggan

Wartime hardship and family strife
in an idyllic Cornish village

**MEREO**
Cirencester

## Mereo Books

1A The Wool Market Dyer Street Cirencester Gloucestershire GL7 2PR
An imprint of Memoirs Publishing www.mereobooks.com

Roscroggan: 978-1-86151-226-0

First published in Great Britain in 2014
by Mereo Books, an imprint of Memoirs Publishing

The address for Memoirs Publishing Group Limited can be found at
www.memoirspublishing.com

The Memoirs Publishing Group Ltd Reg. No. 7834348

The Memoirs Publishing Group supports both The Forest Stewardship Council® (FSC®) and
the PEFC® leading international forest-certification organisations. Our books carrying both the
FSC label and the PEFC® and are printed on FSC®-certified paper. FSC® is the only
forest-certification scheme supported by the leading environmental organisations including
Greenpeace. Our paper procurement policy can be found at
www.memoirspublishing.com/environment

Typeset in 11/17pt Bembo
by Wiltshire Associates Publisher Services Ltd. Printed and bound in Great Britain by
Printondemand-Worldwide, Peterborough PE2 6XD

To Fred, Fran, Margaret, Philip, Anne, Michael and Ray.
In loving memory of Frank and Dave.

# ACKNOWLEDGEMENTS

My thanks to my dear husband Eric for his patience and the technical support I so sorely needed at times. Also to my good friend Rosemary Aitken, author of many great books, for her professional and literary help and guidance, and for steering me into the path of Memoirs Publishing.

Finally to Chris Newton and Tony Tingle at Memoirs for their prompt response, advice and assistance in bringing my work to fruition.

# FOREWORD

Bangs! Shattering glass! Louder bangs! What's happening? I'm afraid! I call for Mummy, then Daddy. Nobody comes! More noise! I'm hurting all over.

I hide under the bedclothes. Then I hear Daddy's voice. "Get out, quickly now!" I grab his hand, and we hurry to Mummy. She is in her bed with all my brothers and my little sister sitting on it. There is a huge bang. Everyone cries out, and my eight-month-old baby sister Margaret is thrown out of her cot. Thank Heaven, Daddy catches her before she lands in all the glass bits scattered over the floor.

Now it is quiet. A man's voice asks if anybody is hurt. Daddy says "No, and how did you get in to the house?"

"I'm an ARP warden" says the man. "Your doors and windows are down, Mr Hugo, you can't stay in there any longer. You and the family will have to leave. If the German planes come back tonight, you're all in danger!"

# CHAPTER 1

Roscroggan, at last! After miles and miles, with legs and feet aching from the never-ending walk, we had arrived. There had been no sirens warning of air raids during our long trek. We wanted no more of the exploding windows and doors we had had in the early hours of the morning back in Penryn, near the Cornish port of Falmouth. They had finally driven us from our home, and we were seeking safety in Aunt Evelyn's house. It was 14th May 1941.

We had walked through other villages we had never seen before. My nine-year-old brother Frank, the next oldest to me, asked Dad why there were no signposts, and was told that because we were at war, the names of places could not be indicated - if the enemy invaded, it would help to confuse them.

Now it was almost dark, and so quiet, with no wind; not even the trees surrounding the cottages rustled. We had never been to Aunt Evelyn's house before, and I hoped Dad could find it OK.

He lifted my youngest brother, five-year-old David, from his makeshift seat on the bedding piled into our long galvanised tin bath. The bath was sitting on top of lots of other belongings which we had frantically rescued from the house and stuffed into Margaret's pram, to be desperately pushed along by Dad and the boys.

Mum, who had travelled on the bus to Camborne (the nearest town to Roscroggan) with baby Margaret, must have heard us arrive, because she came out to meet us. She took four-year-old Frances out of the pushchair, leaving me to remove the bundles of clothes tied to its handle and fold the chair before taking it indoors. I breathed a sigh of relief. We were at the right house.

Frank and Frederick, my two other brothers, who were nine and seven, had pots and pans tied round them with string and were as tired as I was. I had often been in charge of the pushchair when we all went out together, but I'd never done so for such a long way nor walked so far before.

Aunt Evelyn's house was small, two rooms upstairs and two down, but she had said that as long as we were prepared to 'push away with it' we were welcome to stay for a day or two. She gave us bread with home-made jam and clotted cream on it, saffron buns and cocoa drinks. We children were all wrapped up in the bedding we'd brought with us and we went to bed on the floor in the front downstairs room. Mum and Dad were given the back room upstairs. The three cousins we'd never met, we were told, were already in bed in Aunty's room upstairs. Aunty said we should remember that the address was Red River Cottages. I wondered if there was a red river and if so, what it looked like. Was it really red?

I was very tired, but as the grown-ups were still awake and talking in the kitchen next door I hadn't been able to get off to sleep immediately.

Aunt Evelyn, my dad's sister – I had been named after her - said to him, "Those poor mites must be worn out, Fred. That was fifteen miles you walked. You should have found someone with a van to bring you all."

Dad told her he hadn't had time. The council official had said our house was unsafe and with the possibility of the German bombers returning that night we'd had to move out quickly.

The next morning, as soon as I awoke, I got up and peeped out of the window into Aunty's garden. I could hear chickens clucking away somewhere outside but I couldn't see them. I dressed quickly; I could hardly wait to go out. Then Mum came to wake us. She was pleased to see I had got myself up already, but said I should have washed before I had dressed.

In the kitchen, Aunty was stirring something in a saucepan. Mum took me into another small back room, which she called the scullery. There was a table with a bowl on it and pink flannel and soap for me to wash, and a white towel lay beside it. Before she let me use anything she took me outside the back door into the garden and walked with me to the end of a path, where there was a small wooden shed with a lavatory inside. She indicated that I was to use it. I asked why it was so far away from the house, because at Penryn we hadn't had to go outside. She said that it was normal in the country and I should remember where it was, because I would have to go on my own from then on.

On the way back I saw the chickens. There were several in a run with a big shed at the end of it. I made up my mind that I would offer to help collect the eggs sometime. I had done it before, when staying with my grandmother.

We had porridge and some bread and jam for breakfast. I was surprised to find that our three cousins had already been out playing somewhere, and Aunt Evelyn introduced them; Lizzie (real name Frances), who was the eldest, at nine, called after my mother, and her two brothers, Jimmy, seven, and Percy, five.

They were told who we were and asked to take care of us, because we were new to Roscroggan. They were asked to show us the fields where we could play, and we were warned about not going too close to the tin streams nearby and to stay together until we could manage on our own. I was the eldest at ten, but I promised I'd take notice of my cousins. So I was a bit worried when as soon as we were away from the house, Jimmy grabbed my brothers and said, "Come on boys, we've got things to show you you'll never believe", and off they ran up the track, leaving us two girls to follow. When I complained to Lizzie, she laughed, saying, "Oh it doesn't matter, my brothers never take any notice of Ma, they always go off without me, they pair don't like sharing with girls".

We too set off up the short track but we walked, stepping over a narrow stream running along level with the wide exit gateway. Then we passed a big house and we were out on the main road, on a hill. Fifty yards up the hill on the right was a church; 'Roscroggan Methodist Church' was carved out in the stone over the top. Lower down, in smaller writing, was an engraved foundation stone which said 'laid in 1888'. The building next door was smaller, with 'Sunday School' written over the door. Lizzie saw me looking. "The Sunday school is closed" she said. "It needs a lot of repairs and they haven't got the money, but the church is open so we use that for Sunday school in the afternoon and the grown-ups use it for church in the evening. Do you go to Sunday school?"

"Oh yes", I told her, "We used to go every week. Frank and me have some books we've got for regular attendance at Penryn."

"Good," Frances said, "I hope when you get a house of your own you won't go too far away, then you can come here with us."

There was a low wall in front of the church with a gateway entrance marked by two tall granite pillars and a short path up to the church door. All along the top of the wall were black lumps about four inches apart. The Sunday School entrance had been treated in the same way. I asked Lizzie what the lumps were.

"Tar," she answered. "There used to be iron railings all along the walls but they were taken away to make guns for the war effort, and they filled in the holes with tar. They took both the gates as well. And when you go to town you will notice none of the houses have any gates."

# CHAPTER 2

We sat on the church wall and Lizzie asked why we had come to Roscroggan. I explained what had happened at Penryn. She thought it was frightening to have so much damage done to the house that we couldn't live in it any more but she said they'd had nothing like that at Roscroggan, so maybe we should stay there always. She said it would be nice for her to have another girl to play with and it might be safer for all of us not to have to go anywhere else, and weren't we lucky that Dad was at home to help us all?

I asked about her dad. I knew he was in the Royal Navy, but didn't know where he was. They did get letters, she said, but they were censored and no addresses were allowed on them. Lizzie thought her mum had a secret address she wrote to and her letters were passed on to his ship.

Between the wall we sat on and the front wall of the church was an area of grass. Lots of daisies grew there. Lizzie picked several of them and showed me how to make a daisy chain. I'd never done that before and found it difficult because my fingernails were not long enough to split the stems.

We talked more about some of the things we liked to do for fun, and of when we'd lived at Penryn. Then she pointed out a lane on the other side of the road running parallel with the hill but behind tall hedging which blocked our view of it. She said the lane led up past another house to an estate named Mount Whistle, which was owned by a family named Kelly. The lane ended at a main road leading to the north cliffs to the left, and to Pool, near Redruth, to the right. She said Mr Kelly senior was a Justice of the Peace. He owned lots of land, and together with several grown-up sons grew a variety of vegetables and soft fruits. There was also a daughter who taught music. Lizzie thought she might like to play the piano when she was older.

Then the boys came running down the hill, and Lizzie suggested we went in for dinner. Indoors, we discovered that Dad had gone out to look around the area to see if there were any empty houses we might be able to rent.

There wasn't room around the table for us all to sit down together, so we had to eat in two lots. There was an appetising smell of stew, and my mum said we were to eat all we were given as a lot of effort had gone into making it. I'm sure we did do it justice, as very little was left.

We had egg custard for pudding, which reminded me to mention about collecting the eggs. Aunty said she always did that herself a long time before anyone else was up in the mornings because she liked a fresh egg for her breakfast, but if I woke up early enough to join her I could help. But somehow I never managed to wake up before anyone else.

When the boys went off again in the afternoon, Lizzie and I took Frances out in her pushchair, this time going down the hill and along the road for a little way to a crossroads. On the left of us was a large white building. Lizzie said it used to be a chapel but it wasn't used any more. On our right was a lane. We turned into it. A few steps in stood a bungalow, where a lady was in her garden picking washing in from her line and dropping it into a wicker flasket. She called to Lizzie, "Are you looking for primroses?"

"Hullo, Miss Turner, yes we would like to take some home to Mummy and my aunty" Lizzie replied.

The lady came to her gate, which was painted black and made of wood. "And who is this young lady?" she asked.

"This is my cousin, Evelyn, and her baby sister Frances, they have come a long way with all their family to stay with us until her da can find them another house to live in. Theirs has been damaged in the war."

"Gracious me, your mummy has her hands full Lizzie, tell her that if she needs any help not to be afraid to ask me. I go up to town twice a week with Merry and the jingle, I can always bring shopping back for her."

"Who are Merry and the jingle?" I asked when we'd left the lady and made our way further down the lane.

"Merry is Miss Turner's pony, and the jingle is her two-wheeled cart" Lizzie said. "She has a sister and a brother and they all live in that nice little house. It's called The Bungalow. They are very kind people and you'll see them in church on Sunday."

We did find some wild flowers, primroses and violets. It was wonderful to be able to pick flowers that didn't belong to anyone. I was afraid we would get into trouble, but nobody came to shout at us.

Frank and Frederick came home with tales of their adventures. They had gone with Jimmy and Percy to investigate a tunnel which they said ran under a farm and out towards some very high chimney stacks which they thought were something to do with the tin mines a couple of miles away.

We did go out together sometimes during the next few days and enjoyed watching the animals in the fields. We learned the difference between cows and horses. Although our cousins were surprised at us not knowing certain things, they didn't mind teaching us.

The weather always seemed warm for the few weeks we lived at Aunty's cottage. Some days she packed up sandwiches, saffron buns and lemonade in a bottle for picnics. My mum said we were making a lot of work, but Aunty said "Let them be Frances, they are only kids, and if kids can't have fun while they're young when can they? And who knows how long this war will last?"

One day Mum and Aunt Evelyn made pasties and saffron buns and all except Dad, who was still searching for another house, walked to Portreath beach, about two miles away. Further on up the hill on the right past the church was a gateway into a field with a wide track leading to somewhere called 'Sleepy Hollow'. I liked that name.

After passing some very smart houses and a green triangle of grass on the left, there was a road which Aunty said led down between some dark-leaved rhododendron trees to Tehidy Tuberculosis Hospital. Here she said the patients lived outside in their beds, except when it poured with rain.

Then we turned left again and the next stretch was another hill, but as it too was countryside with lots of trees and hedges with wild flowers, I found it more interesting. Lizzie told me there were several hidden entrances to Tehidy through woods, with squirrels living in the trees who weren't afraid of humans. As I had never seen a real squirrel, only pictures in books, we planned to go there one day.

The remainder of the walk was on the level and ended at the top of a steep hill overlooking the beach and the sea. It was a smaller beach than the one we used to visit at Falmouth, but we couldn't wait to get to it. On such a glorious day the sea was a lovely greeny blue with small white-topped waves lapping the shore line.

The boys cheered and ran ahead, and by the time the rest of us got to them after dragging the pram over the sand they were stripped off and ready to run into the water. I had no costume, so I had to stay on the beach. The sand was warm and we discovered lots of rock pools. Lizzie showed me how to find limpets and remove them from the rocks to which they clung, and by lifting up the seaweed we discovered tiny fish and baby crabs hidden away.

Way off the beach, some distance out in the water, was a huge rock. Aunty called it Gull Rock, and said that at weekends young men held swimming races out to and around it. She made us promise never to attempt it.

What a wonderful day that turned out to be. We were all tired, I was tingling from the sun on my fair skin and we were all ready for our beds when we reached home again. Dad had not found us a new house, but he was pleased to hear of our lovely day.

A few days later Aunt Evelyn's landlady came and took Mum and Dad to see a cottage for which she was also an agent, not far away near the tin stream works. She explained that the cottage was one of four, three of which were lived in. It had been declared derelict and needed a lot of work done to it to make it fit for us to live in. I was told to take care of the young ones and not to get in Aunt Evelyn's way.

Next day a letter came from the Army. Dad explained to us that in view of our homelessness he had been given compassionate leave for another three weeks. He went to the local council, who said they had no spare houses or flats but agreed that if he could do something in the way of improvements to the cottage he'd been offered (they understood it belonged to a local doctor), he would be able to rent the property.

Apart from learning some new words and losing some of our shyness, the boys and I learned what work was all about from then on. While the boys helped Dad, I had to stay with Mum to get the cottage cleaned up. It was very dirty. The floors in the kitchen and front room were made of cement, and because it had not been lived in for a long time, there were dead insects all over the place. Lots of rubbish had come down the chimneys and the big black Cornish range we were going to have to use for cooking was grey, thick with dust and ash and in places brown with rust. The brass knobs were black with not having been cleaned for a long time. Huge cobwebs hung in every room and spiders ran about everywhere.

The first day we entered we discovered there were only two bedrooms for eight of us to share. Mum and Dad planned to sleep in the downstairs front room. Down two steps at the back of the kitchen there was an extra building, a dark and dirty part of an empty unused attached property. This became Dad's workshop, our coalhouse and a source of timber as he and the boys tore down ceilings and ripped up the upstairs floorboards and any other useful articles to repair the cottage. They also made small items of furniture, backless benches, chairs etc.

No water was laid on to the cottages, so we had to fetch it from an underground pipe (later I was told this was called a chute), in a field about five hundred yards away. The lane to the pipe was behind the tin stream works, which were cut off from anyone using the lane by a six-foot wooden fence. Because we had to go down the lane to fetch water, we soon found that that part of the fence was the rear wall of the carpentry workshops and employees' dinner or 'croust' house.

The large tin bath we had carried from Penryn had been

pushed into Aunt Evelyn's big garden shed. Dad got it out, and using the baby's pram again, he brought it to the cottage. It still contained lots of useful things, including some of our clothes, bedclothes and curtains. He had already got his tools from it.

Underneath it and in the bottom of the pram were all the plates and dishes, with the knives, forks and spoons. Once all these things had been taken in and stowed away in the kitchen and we had discovered a large larder type cupboard under the stairs for them, we found we hadn't got many utensils to carry the water in, especially no buckets!

# CHAPTER 3

A couple of days later, while we children got on with the cleaning, Mum and Dad went to Camborne to do some shopping. When they returned they said they had arranged for the rest of our furniture, the undamaged beds, tables and chairs, some cupboards and the heavy iron saucepans we had left behind at Penryn to be brought by horse and cart. The man would also bring us some buckets and things to fetch water in.

Between bath nights the bath was to live outside the only door of the cottage, collecting rainwater from a downpipe fixed under the roof, or be filled every day from the chute in the field by us children - even the younger ones were expected to carry small jugs full. The warm, dry weather we'd been having since living at Roscroggan did not give us children any hope of a break from fetching water.

Having no water laid on meant no sanitation. The four lavatories, housed in one terraced block, with individual compartments and boltable doors, were at least two hundred yards away past the neighbour's cottages and up a rise behind the properties. This seemed like a mile to us children when having to go in the dark on our own.

Inside they consisted of nothing more than a box with a hinged lid, into which was placed a large lavatory bucket. Across this was a wooden plank with a hole over the bucket. We learned that they were known as thunder-boxes. The boys and I were given the job of emptying ours, always on dark nights, into a local stream some distance from the cottages. With so many in the family it was a frequent and horrible job. Occasionally I would be given a jug containing soapy water and Jeyes Fluid, a black strong-smelling disinfectant, to wash the bucket out. When I grumbled I was told that cleaning was women's work. There was no point in my saying I was only a girl!

There was no such thing as special lavatory paper like we had at school. We had to cut newspaper into six-inch squares, and after making a hole in a corner, we would thread string through and hang it on the back of the lavatory door.

Frederick reminds me of another nasty connection. The old man who lived two doors away would often frighten us children by using our lavatory and not bolting the door. This was to save him the trouble of emptying his own. I also had to use Jeyes Fluid, together with a white square block of Monkey brand stone, to scrub out the lavatory floor and the large granite front doorstep of the cottage.

Our immediate next-door neighbour on the left as we went up our garden path waited until our whole family had moved into the cottage before coming to make herself known to us. Her name was Mrs Mankee. Her husband was a tin miner who had gone to the Gold Coast to work. They had five children,

Joan, Jean, Garfield, Freddie, and David. The boys and my brothers sometimes got to play together, but Joan was older than me and nearly ready for going out to work. Jean was Frank's age. She didn't have responsibilities such as younger family to look after or shopping to do after school as I did, so I wasn't very well liked because I could not join in their games.

My sister Frances tells of sitting on the doorstep with one of the Mankee girls, who gave her a doll. As she had never owned one before she was really happy, but then the girl spoiled it all by telling her there was no Father Christmas. She was heartbroken, and not very keen on the girl afterwards.

Soon the work on the cottage was finished and a couple of people from the Council came to look at it and agreed that Dad had made it good enough for us to live in until we could find somewhere better. It still only consisted of four rooms.

I noticed that the stairs had actually been moved from what was to be the kitchen into the front room, thus leaving room in the kitchen against the inner dividing wall for the larder-type cupboard and the long backless form that Dad and the boys had made.

At the top of the stairs stood our large dark brown chest of drawers, now freshly painted, with three full-width drawers and two halves at the top. Mum always had a white lace runner on it, although because the top was shiny with the varnish Dad had used it often slipped off on to the floor between the chest and the wall. The front wall had a window and recess, and a small brown and cream cane table stood there.

In the front left corner was a tallboy. This too contained three drawers, but the top consisted of a two-door cupboard. This item was Mum and Dad's sole property, and woe betide anyone interfering with it. I never did know what it contained.

Against the side wall was a double bed. In those days double beds were only 4ft wide, singles 2ft 6ins, although some singles were slightly bigger at 3ft, enabling two children to sleep together. The double beds also had a bolster, which was double the length of a normal pillow and lay in a fitted bolster case under the two pillows.

In the back left corner was a single bed. At the foot of it a large black trunk contained the boys' clothes. Then came the doorway in the dividing wall to my room. On the right, which was the high side of the room as we entered, was my bed. At the foot a small cupboard contained all us girls' underclothes. A small window in the wall was directly over the kitchen. In the lowest part of this attic room was the larger of the single beds where Frances and Margaret slept together. This room was always warm from the heat of the kitchen below.

All the beds had black rails head and foot, with brass knobs on all four corner posts. The mattresses contained flock. The sheets were cotton twill, and took a lot of drying on washday. I don't remember how often the grey woollen blankets got washed, but I do recall them being hung out to air occasionally. Over the top of the blanket was a bedspread, a thin cotton cover with a washed-out flower pattern.

In the front room downstairs, apart from Mum and Dad's double bed against the inner wall, there was a bedside cabinet each side of the bed. By a window in the outer wall stood a small cane table, the same as upstairs. A small fire grate was in the opposite wall. On either side of the grate were recesses which had once been cupboards, but Dad had removed the doors and shelving, lined them to keep them dry and made curtains for both. Now all the family's best clothes hung in them. In those days best clothes were worn on Sundays and special days out only. I've often wondered what sort of picture we made, five of us, fair hair shining, especially Frank and me who were real 'white tops', with well-polished shoes and dressed in our Sunday best trooping out to Sunday School those first few weeks at Roscroggan.

The kitchen, now containing a brightly polished blackleaded Cornish range, with all brasses gleaming, had the only door to the cottage, in the same wall. A window was set into the top half of the door. The kitchen was furnished with a large scrub top table pushed up tight to the wall, over which a cupboard was recessed containing all the pots and pans. This too had a curtain instead of doors.

A large dark wooden-armed high-backed chair stood next to the backless form. This was Dad's chair. Against the other wall were several ordinary kitchen chairs.

We were advised that the address was Number 2, Tehidy Mill Cottages, Roscroggan, Camborne, Cornwall. The rent was to be three shillings and sixpence per month (17p, in present-day money).

With the work finished, Dad had to return to the Army. He

was sorry to leave us but he said we had a comfortable place to live in comparison to some people up the country. We promised to be good and help Mum until he came home again.

# CHAPTER 4

There was no electricity or gas at the cottage. Paraffin lamps and candles supplied the lighting, and the cooking was done on and in the Cornish range.

Mum was a good plain cook. We had nourishing stews, pot roasts and pies, often made with rabbit. This was many years before myxomatosis was introduced and in those days neighbours' husbands were able to go out in the fields catching them.

Meat being rationed, we had corned beef dishes such as cottage pies, 'bubble and squeak' (cabbage and potato mashed and fried) and corned beef hash. We still managed to have pasties occasionally and when the weather permitted we were allowed to sit out on the step to eat them. Because they came straight from the oven they were wrapped around with newspaper to prevent us burning our hands.

One amusing incident that comes to mind was when a neighbour dropped in with a rabbit. He had obviously called in somewhere for a drink before reaching us and wasn't too steady on his feet. Frank opened the door, recognised him, and stepped back to let him in.

The man propped himself against the wall beside the range and holding the dead rabbit up level with his face he shook his head at it, saying "Oh you poor, poor, beddy bunny, oh, you poor, poor…" He repeated this while slowly sliding down the wall until he lay flat out asleep on the floor. Frank went to the man's home close to Aunt Evelyn's cottage and came back with his two grown-up sons, who carried him home. This incident was never mentioned again. Obviously it wasn't done to talk about a neighbour who came bearing gifts, even if it was comical!

We did occasionally have fish from the grocer's, but it was never fresh. It came dried in large pieces, or often the whole fish with head, tail and innards removed, it was very salty. Almost grey in colour, it had to be soaked in water overnight before cooking. None of us children liked it, but in those days you ate what you were given. The boys and I used to pull faces at each other if we smelt it cooking. I learnt that it came mainly from Brittany.

Being the eldest, I remembered going to the quay at Penryn and buying fresh mackerel and herrings from the fishermen returning from sea with their catch. In fact I had done so only a few days before leaving. I have recently read an account of what food was like during those days, and one lady likened the dried fish to eating a flannelette sheet. I wonder how she knew that?

Dried apple rings cooked and served with hot custard were our pudding, although once harvest time came round we were sometimes given large bags of fresh apples by growers, which we ate instead. We were also sent out to pick blackberries when in season.

Rice puddings cooked in the oven of the Cornish range were a favourite too, especially to me. I was always ready to fight for the lovely brown skin tasting of nutmeg, which I would volunteer to grate over the top prior to it going into the oven. It is still a treat I allow myself occasionally.

The rule in the house was that you were not allowed to have sweet food at teatime until you had eaten at least one piece of bread. Sometimes there was no butter or margarine to spread on it, so we had either dripping (beef fat, saved and allowed to cool and harden from the cooked joint), sugar sprinkled over it or thinly-poured condensed milk. It was also a rule that you ate nothing between meals. Obviously with such a large family it would have been impossible to ever clear the table of food.

One other rule we had at mealtimes - you could not leave the table while you were eating. Every bit of what you had on your plate had to be eaten before you moved, and then you asked, "Please may I leave the table?" Mum or Dad would look around the table and if anyone still had food to eat you would be told to wait until they had finished. Many a time I remember sitting there willing somebody to hurry up and finish so that I could get back to whatever I wanted to do next.

My sister Frances recalls Mum going to town to do the weekly shop, taking the empty pram. One or more of us children went with her, the eldest of us staying to look after the youngest. She always went to Camborne. There were no buses, so the two miles had to be walked both ways.

On other days Frank, Frederick and I had to go especially to buy potatoes. They were rationed to one gallon per customer, a measurement no longer in common use today with pre-packaging, and we had to visit separate shops to buy enough for our large family.

One day I was put on a Marigold bus in Camborne and told to go back to Penryn to one of the shops Mum used to deal with and pay them some money Mum had left owing when we had moved so quickly. When we got to Lanner the bus turned around to go back the way we had come. I was so upset at having to go home with the debt still not paid I started to cry. I was the one child in the family who seemed always to anger Mum without meaning to.

A lady passenger asked what was upsetting me. When I told her about the trouble I should be in at home she assured me that the bus had to go so far back on the same road to pick up people living there, and that it would be heading back on the correct road for Falmouth later. I was so relieved when this turned out to be the case.

While I was in the Penryn shop I heard people talking about another air attack on Penryn and Falmouth. Although some bombs had dropped into the sea, houses had been machine-gunned and much more damage done. I also learned that on the night our house had been damaged, eighteen people had been killed and as many more had been injured. I was pleased we were safely living at Roscroggan. I remembered to tell Mum what I'd heard when I got home.

Frances recalls bath nights in front of the Cornish range.

Because we used our large galvanised bungalow bath, which took so much water, we had to bath the younger children in twos. There was always a bit of grumbling if the first pair took too long, as the water wouldn't be as warm or as clean when the second pair had their turn.

# CHAPTER 5

The Tin Stream Works were very close to the cottages. At the entrance to the lane where we fetched the water there was a large wooden hatchway in the side of a stone building which was opened up by the workmen every other day to permit lorries filled with a dark grey clay-like material to unload on to a platform in front of it.

The workmen (three names we remember are Gordon Berriman, Harry Jennings and Garfield Laity) used long-handled Cornish shovels to transfer the material to settling tables just inside the building. Frank remembers the owner, a Mr Harold Rodda, and his son Donald, who also worked in the office, having a Ford 8 or 10 car in 1941.

These settling tables were large, round and sloped downwards to a holed centre. They were made solely of wood, and around the top was a channel about four inches wide filled with angled butterfly winged nuts. Automatic hammers attached to overhead workings continually, night and day, banged against the side of the settling tables, with a thump-thump-thump sound.

Water too was fed on to the clay. As they shook, the tin,

which was heavier than the waste, was separated and the waste disappeared down into the hole. Later the heavy tin ore was shovelled into bags and taken away by lorry to the smelting works. The wet clay made the platform extremely sticky and dangerous, and we were warned to stay clear of it.

A short distance away along the narrow unmade road were six 'tailing lakes', so called because they contained the residue or 'tailings,' not considered worth processing by the larger companies, such as the mines a couple of miles up the road. These lakes were fifteen to twenty feet deep, and were kept in a state of agitation by the 'streamers', men who walked between each lake carrying extremely long poles with a box-like structure at the end, which they pumped and pressed down continuously into the slimy red bottom of the lake. The men could often be heard singing and calling to one another. Incidentally this tomato-coloured tin slime was the reason for the 'Red' of 'Red River'.

The walls between the streams nearest the road were about twelve inches wide. I could walk along them easily, though I was no gymnast, but quite often girls as well as boys could be seen doing handstands on them. Mum threatened me with a hiding if she caught me doing that.

The neighbours on the other side of us were very quiet. We learned there was an old lady who lay all the time in her bed, a man, whom we understood was known as Jamsie, though we saw very little of him, and a daughter whom we were told to call Miss Williams.

We had only been in the cottage a month or two when the old lady died. Miss Williams came to ask my mother if we would like to come and see the old lady now she was at peace. I was very curious about the subject of what happened when people were dead, having heard about the war casualties, and gladly went with Mum. To me it seemed as if the lady was asleep, so obviously it didn't hurt to die. I asked Mum why Miss Williams was crying and was told to be quiet because I didn't understand what I was seeing.

Then one day when we came home from school the Williams' cottage was empty. I was told that Miss Williams had been taken into service (apparently this was a job where the worker lived in at the house and only went home for one half day per week). Her brother, the man who lived there, was put into the workhouse and one day we could go to see him. I didn't like the sound of that because I had read a book at school where little boys from a workhouse were taken out to go to work up people's chimneys (possibly Charles Kingsley's *The Water Babies*), so I was a bit afraid of what would happen to us if we went visiting in there.

We were now closer to the old man and his wife and family, and they were not nice neighbours. He often came home late at night singing at the top of his voice. The Mankee children said he was always drunk when he'd been to a market town somewhere buying and selling horses. We understood he was from gypsy stock. His one redeeming feature was that he always wore clean, well-polished, brown riding boots.

One evening he frightened the younger children by bursting into our kitchen waving a big stick in the air and shouting at Mum. Mum made the children hide under the kitchen table until the old man got his stick tangled with a sticky fly paper hanging from our ceiling. When he left struggling to free himself of the gooey mess, his wife screamed and shouted obscenities and started throwing stones at our door, the top half of which was glass – luckily she didn't break it.

Up until then we didn't know what being drunk meant. We weren't familiar with anything to do with alcohol.

His wife spent a lot of time outside her cottage washing their clothes in a rainwater barrel with cold water in it. We never saw the water emptied out and fresh put in. She continually sang in a high-pitched, squeaky voice 'You'll never miss your mother till she's gone', 'Sell me a ticket to heaven', and 'In The Sweet By and By'.

She was well known in the area and suspected of stealing clothes from people's washing lines at night. We were constantly hearing tales from neighbours. Even as far away as Camborne she was known as 'Moonlight Moggy'.

Mum always had a lot of washing to do She used a large black oval iron boiler with a handle each end, and some of the iron saucepans to heat up the water on the Cornish range; then she poured it into a small galvanised bath that rested on the kitchen table in which she did the washing.

Generally Mum used a hard green block of soap called Puritan, yellow Sunlight or a dark pink carbolic, but soap was rationed, like most things. We had coupons allocated to us according to what ration books we had. Each book was worth four coupons per month. These were worth one coupon each. We could also purchase a three-ounce bar of toilet soap, Lifebuoy, Lux or Pears plus half an ounce of liquid soap, also equalling one coupon.

There was soft soap and soap flakes for special delicate fabrics, but we never bought anything like that. One item we did buy and use was Reckitts Blue. This was a small square, about the size of an Oxo cube, of compacted blue powder. It was usually put into a piece of cloth screwed tightly at the top and dipped into the third rinse of all the white laundry. Care had to be taken not to leave it in the whites too long or they'd all be far too blue instead of simply enhancing the whiteness.

Sometimes a scrubbing brush was necessary on the collars and cuffs. The washed clothes were always hung out in the fresh air to dry. Many articles required starching; hot water starch was needed for tablecloths, shirts and blouses, but cold water starch was used for collars and cuffs. I never got trusted with the blueing or starching. Except for baby wear I never remember washing hanging indoors to dry.

I didn't like washdays because of the ironing that came afterwards. I always had to do a lot of it with a boxed iron when Mum and Dad went to the pictures on Saturdays. It was a hot and dangerous job for someone as young as me. The iron was triangular, like all irons, and consisted of an iron box with a wooden handle. It contained a small lump of metal in the same shape. This lump had to be put in the fire to get very hot, and when it was hot enough it had to be lifted out of the fire with a special piece of metal with a hook in the end and placed in the box. A small door in the straight end of the iron was dropped down, trapping the hot metal inside. It made a sort of 'knick–knack' sound. I used it until the lump got cool and was not doing its job. Of course we had two lumps, so while I used one the other was in the fire getting hot.

On Sunday evenings there was always extra water needed ready for Monday's washday, especially if there'd been no rain for several days. Frank, Frederick and I had to fetch that when we came home from church. Margaret recalls going for water one time when a man shouted at her. When she looked up, he was on a hill pointing what looked like a gun at her. Terrified, she left the bucket and ran home screaming.

One of the old couple's children, a four-year-old, died. The coroner's inquest said it was as a result of drinking paraffin or methylated spirit. Frances told me that once the child had fallen into a stream. Frances pulled her out and the child seemed not to have come to any harm. Taking her home, the mother was not concerned at all.

Some days after the child died the mother came to our house to ask Mum if she could give her a blanket to wrap its body in. Mum gave her a very nice one with a pink ribbon on the edge. On the day of the funeral the mother rushed after the horse and cart, whose driver was the undertaker, demanding the return of the blanket, as she said it was too good to throw away!

The woman never went to the funeral, although I understand that in those days it wasn't as common for women to attend funerals as it is today. Mum was quite upset, and she cried when the mother said she would only miss the milk tokens she used to get for the dead child.

We had a lot of trouble with those people. They threw dirty water all over our kitchen floor when we left the door open one day. One evening Dad was away, of course, and Mum had gone out. The woman was outside our door screaming and swearing. Frank opened the door and threw a jug of water over her, telling her to clear off back to her own house. The old man put a clothes prop through the glass panel in the top of our door in retaliation. A short while later the woman was sent to prison for breaking into locked premises and stealing money.

The man had a dog, a black Labrador cross. One day while his wife was still in prison it got out and tore into Mr Mankee's garden, killing the children's pet rabbit. Mr Mankee, having recently returned from the Gold Coast after mining out there, had bought himself a car, a white MG sports model. When he came home from town and learned about the rabbit he went over to complain. As a result, the man started kicking the new car. Mr Mankee turned the car around and drove away, and returned later with a police car following. Two policemen took a much quieter old man away. The empty, dirty cottage was boarded up, and we never saw that old couple again at Roscroggan.

# CHAPTER 6

The first day school we were sent to (I attended it for a few days only) was at Roskear, near Camborne, about a mile and a half away. We had to cross one of the tailing lakes by a narrow wooden bridge just wide enough to take a small child's pushchair (with no rails to hold on to it was scary) and up a rough stony track that ended outside of the home of Butcher Williams, who became our butcher (he wasn't a killer!)

Then into a narrow lane, at the end of which they crossed the main road at the junction between Tuckingmill, a small community built around the Bickford Smith Gunpowder Factory, a gasworks and more tin streaming works, and Roskear itself, on into the school. It took children up to the age of eleven. Frances still believes it was at least five miles.

Margaret remembers it as a long walk. She still carries a scar on her leg which she received from climbing a wall. She had been forbidden to climb by Mum, so Frances got blamed for letting her do it. She also remembers her last teacher there, because of the bright red nail varnish she always wore.

Frank recalls his early days at Roskear School. The teacher

refused to accept that he was simply called Frank and insisted it had to be short for Franklyn or Francis. Several raps over the knuckles finally elicited a note from Mum, and his name was recognised.

The class had been asked to write an essay on something they'd done on holiday. Frank chose to describe a weekend camping in Tehidy Woods, including going to Portreath to catch small crustaceans to cook over the camp fire.

Frank's essay, when read to his teacher and the class, earned him compliments on content, setting out and the sense of adventure he'd managed to imply in the reading. When it was handed over however, his teacher grew very angry, ranting and raving before finally throwing the paper back in disgust. It transpired that he was unimpressed with Frank having printed every word instead of doing it in proper joined-up writing. Finally Frank got the opportunity to explain that he had never been taught the art of 'proper writing' at Penryn. The teacher planned on writing to Penryn School complaining at their failure to provide this essential skill. Meanwhile Frank was to stay for a half an hour after school each day until he could write to his teacher's satisfaction.

In the last but one year, Roskear pupils had to take the eleven plus preliminary exam. If they passed it they were allowed to take the eleven plus final. Passing the final meant they either went to the Camborne County School for girls or the Redruth Grammar School for boys.

When I had left Penryn I had got a rash on my arms and

legs. The teacher had sent me to the doctor, who said it was called impetigo and was something brought to the area by up-country strangers. He said it was infectious and I wasn't to go to school again until it was cleared up, so although I had already taken the preliminary exam and passed it at Penryn, because of my absence due to the rash I arrived at Roskear School too late for the eleven-plus final.

At that time I had to wear thick bandages and long black stockings and was not permitted to tell anyone why. One day a man working on the tin-streams saw me fetching water, and asked me why I wasn't at school. I didn't tell him, but I told Mum. A few days later the same man gave her a tin of ointment, a soft pink cream called St James's Balm. He said I was to bath every day, put on lots of this stuff and not cover up the rash but let the air get to it. It wasn't long before it cleared up.

We always had a tin of 'St James's' in the cupboard afterwards, together with iodine and Vaseline. The government supplied orange juice and cod liver oil, to help make up for the lack of certain nourishing foods in our wartime diet. We also had a large jar of malt and cod liver oil, which most of us loved. Frances reminds me that Dad had a favourite remedy for everything, syrup of figs. Whatever we ailed from he always put it down to our bowels and the need for opening medicine, and syrup of figs was the cure!

In 1942 Mum had given birth to another boy child, Philip, born on Frank's birthday, 14th February, so we now had two Valentine birthdays. The doctor who came to see Mum after the birth said she must not risk having any more children.

At eleven years old I was sent to Basset Road Girls' School in Camborne, a semi-detached property; the other half was a boys' school. The girls were not allowed to mix with the boys. Down the middle of the playground was a double row of back-to-back lavatories. A teacher always stood in the yard at playtime, so there was no way we could peep through the little gap at the end to see what the boys were doing.

I liked my new school, particularly because I had to wear a uniform, a black gymslip with three box pleats back and front (I remember being afraid to sit down in it because of spoiling the pleats), a crisp white blouse with long sleeves, white ankle socks and black shoes. I must confess to a feeling of pride at being dressed as the other girls were. My only complaint was that I was only ever bought lace-up shoes the same as the boys wore, whilst I noticed that my school friends wore button strap shoes, much prettier with the white ankle socks.

The only lesson I wasn't keen on was singing. Miss James, the music teacher, a tall, thin elderly soprano, tried to make me sing in a higher key than I was capable of, and for this purpose she would stop the whole class and call me out in front. When I couldn't perform she would make me stop altogether. I then had to sit at the front and listen, being constantly prodded with her baton to remind me how it should sound.

On Sundays, dressed in our clean clothes, which were kept only for best, we went to Roscroggan Methodist Church and Sunday School. It was cosy and warm. All the pews were shiny and there were small cushions to help us to sit without sliding off. All us children were sent at least once each Sunday but mostly we had to go twice, in the afternoon and again in the evening.

The Sunday school building next door was still not in good repair, so we didn't use it. I became friendly with a lady called Mrs Bassett, who played the organ each week for the evening services. In the afternoons she taught Sunday school. I learned a little about the early days of the building. It had originally been registered as a place of worship in October 1850. There was a small cemetery at the rear of the building.

Mrs Basset was the great granddaughter of Mr William Henry Mitchell of Rosewarne Downs, one of the original Lessees of 1850. In the 1960s a report on this chapel stated that the history of Methodism in this quiet backwater went back a great deal further than 1850. It claimed that the unbroken thread was due to the love and devotion of one family, the Mitchells.

Mrs Bassett lived at the top of the hill, at South Tehidy, next door to a Mr and Mrs Ashton. Together with several other people, all four were Trustees of the Roscroggan Methodist Church. Mr Basset was the door steward. Mrs Bassett said that when I became old enough I could be a Trustee. In the meantime she would help me to learn as much as possible about all I would need to know in later life. She was always very kind to me.

Mr Ashton, as well as being Chief Steward, was a lay preacher. Sometimes when a minister was unavailable for our church he would take the service. He told wonderful stories, often about people he'd met on his travels around the world, but he also enjoyed singing, so often on a Sunday the seventy-five-year-old

Church echoed loudly with the tuneful Sankey hymns we all loved, 'Bringing in the sheaves', 'Trust and obey', 'Count your blessings' and especially the children's favourite 'Jesus wants me for a sunbeam'.

Most of the boys from the village attended and had to take turns pumping air into the organ. It meant one of them would have to sit at the side near the back of the organ, pushing down and pulling up a long wooden lever jutting out from the side until enough air had been pumped into the bellows to allow Mrs Bassett to play.

Occasionally, when the Minister was reading the lesson for the day or preaching his sermon and there was no need to pump the organ, a mischievous boy would have his peashooter handy and the congregation would suffer a rain of newspaper pellets and not realise where they were coming from. When he was finally discovered, the boy concerned was fetched out of the pumping hidey-hole and made to sit beside Mrs Bassett in full view of the whole congregation, while someone who could be trusted not to misbehave pumped the organ.

(At one of the Trustees' meetings in the 1940s they were asked to make a donation to the Churches War Damage Repairs Fund. £5 was suggested. Due to the work required on their own premises they were unable to help. When their own repairs were completed they did contribute, with a donation of just over £2.)

Frank and Frederick were now at Roskear School. Frank had taken the eleven-plus preliminary exam and like me he'd passed. He'd later gone on to pass the scholarship, earning a place at Redruth Grammar School for boys.

Frederick had made friends with Mr and Mrs Ham, owners of the farm nearby, who lived with their daughter and son-in-law, Enid and Freddy Butler. Mr Ham was surprised to learn of such a large family living in the small cottage. They always supplied our milk, eggs and vegetables.

By this time Mum had got friendly with Enid Butler and spent some time helping her with knitting patterns for clothes for her two children. With such a large family we had lots of clothing coupons. Extra to the normal ration book these were small square stamps in paper books, simply named Points Coupon Books, issued by the Government, which people had to give to the shopkeeper as well as money so that they could buy clothes that were on a ration system.

We had more coupons than we needed and, because prices had risen such a lot, we did not have enough money to buy new clothes. Enid shopped in Camborne, where the shops were mainly for families. In Trelowarren Street (the main street) there were five Co-op department stores. Children's clothing including school uniforms, gents' and ladies' outfitters, footwear for everybody, soft furnishings and grocery.

Enid would use our spare coupons, then buy knitting wool for Mum. If she felt something else was also due to Mum when she came home she would load a trug – a flattish garden basket - full of vegetables, fruit & eggs and send Freddy to our house with it. In this way we had certain nice things other people didn't.

Quite often when I was sent to get jugs of milk from the farm there would be none in the dairy ready for sale at that time.

I was quickly taught how to fetch the cows in from the fields, fasten them in their stalls in the barn and milk them. Luckily for me the cows were always ready to give the milk and would have started their homeward trek through the fields toward the farm before I reached them.

Milking was done by hand; there were no milking machines in those days. I sat on a three-legged stool. I was taught to lean toward the cow, rest my forehead against its side, grasp two of the four teats jutting out from the udder under the cow's belly, and gently squeeze and pull alternately. I had to direct the milk into a bucket tilted towards the cow but held firmly between my knees, and when those teats were empty I changed over to the other two and continued until those also seemed empty, when I went to another cow.

In spite of my being shorter than the cows they gave me no trouble. I loved the warmth of them on the cold days. My favourite was Molly, who was long-legged and a rich dark reddish-brown colour. She gave thick creamy milk. Whenever I had to milk them myself, Molly would always be the first. She never flicked her tail over me when I was milking her and often gave me a nudge when I let them out of the barn afterwards. I liked to think she was saying thank you.

The downside of that chore was that I often got into trouble at home for taking too long to fetch the milk, mainly because everyone would be sitting waiting for their evening meal. It made little difference if one of the boys was sent instead, as they too would be told by the farmer, "If you want milk before we've got the cows in, you must get them in yourself." I have tried hard, but I cannot remember if I ever paid for the milk. It could be that our labour paid for it.

If the milking was in progress when we arrived on the farm there would be other jobs while we waited to be served, such as locking up the poultry or collecting eggs; this often involved scouting around the field hedgerows for the ones laid by broody hens who tried hiding them away until they could also bury themselves in the undergrowth and make a nest. Sometimes we'd be given an egg to take home for our tea, but like the small amount of butter allowed on the ration book, it would be taken from us and given to the baby.

At Basset Road School we were taught to cook. One day a week we were marched up the road to the community centre a short distance away, where a lady called Miss Bath, wearing a white duster coat that always seemed too long for her, instructed us.

My first lesson was to make rock cakes. Mum didn't think much of them, saying they were a waste of good ingredients, but my brothers and sisters enjoyed eating them. Miss Bath had a very handsome brother. She had a photograph of him on her desk in his Army officer's uniform, and several of us girls were always ready to run errands to her just to get a glimpse of it.

One day, I remember I was gone 12 at the time, those of us who were at school had a lovely surprise when we got home. Dad was back and would not have to return to the Army again. He did, though, have to join the Home Guard. I seemed to remember him having to go to Camborne in the evenings sometimes, but with shift work at the mine he wasn't always available.

Apparently he had been sent out on manoeuvres with his unit and while he was away another man from Camborne arriving at the same camp had enquired for him. On being told Dad would not be back for a few days and questioned as to his business, the man explained he had worked with Dad some years before in the tin mines of Camborne and Redruth (Dad was twelve years old when he was first employed in the mine). Now the mine this man had recently been working on had closed and other mines in the area were not taking men on, so he'd had to join the Army.

As at this time the government were not calling up people who were capable of working in jobs that helped the war effort, and tin miners were supplying much needed metal for munitions, they were named as one of the exempt services. Dad was ticked off for not mentioning his mining career before he joined the Army and sent home to go back into the mine. As this meant less money coming into the home, our lives were to change again.

My brothers and I were encouraged to get after-school jobs, mainly on the land. I had been found a paper round for a shop at Tuckingmill, which I had to do after school. It was about three miles, mainly Roscroggan, Tehidy, Halgoss and Tolvaddon.

I had no bicycle so I walked, or ran, everywhere. I quite often earned a telling off from customers for not delivering the papers in the morning, but they never got cross enough to cancel. It would not have made much difference, because my bosses were the only shop who delivered anyway. In school holidays I did deliver in the mornings.

From some of the customers I learned of more bomb damage being done in the Falmouth/ Penryn area. As we still had several relatives living in Falmouth I would make certain I remembered the information exactly so as to tell mum when I got home. It seemed that the docks at Falmouth were a prime target for the German air force.

Later I heard Mum telling Dad what I had said. He told her he had learned about the sinking of some ships and there had been men from Falmouth on board. Two of my male cousins were torpedoed while aboard a ship away from English waters. They were picked up by a German ship and held as prisoners of war.

I had several male cousins in the Royal Navy but we heard no news from their families. Two of our female cousins had also joined the services. They were concerned with ENSA, the Entertainments National Service Association.

One Saturday when I was on my way over to the paper shop at Tuckingmill in the morning, I was totalling up the takings in the cash-book whilst walking along; I had not had time to do it before because of chores at home after school on the Friday., I tripped over a low wall and fell, landing about twelve feet down in a dried-up disused tailing lake. I tried to get up, but couldn't stand. Luckily one of the male workers saw what had happened and I was helped into a wheelbarrow and wheeled home.

The boys had a good laugh at my embarrassing arrival back home, but it wasn't so funny when they realised I had sprained both ankles, because they would have to do my chores and Frank would have to do my paper round until I was able to resume my duties again. This was quite a chore for him, as he was always later getting home from school than me due to having to travel home on the bus from Redruth. Frederick was also now at the grammar school.

One day Frank and me went to fetch water. On the way back we stopped to rest, and Frank discovered a large crack in the fencing separating the tin-stream workshop from the lane we were in. He called out and someone inside shouted back to him. He laughed and indicated for me to come and look. He stepped back, making room for me, and I stood on the same spot trying to peer through the crack. Then something hit the woodwork and I don't remember anything more until I heard my mother shouting, "What was she doing?"

Frank's voice said, "Looking through the crack in the fence."

"It serves her right then," my mother said.

I sat up and realised I had been lying on the kitchen floor. Frank saw me move and gave me his hand to help me up. He pulled up a chair, helping me to sit on it. My mother shouted again, "What were you doing? You were sent to fetch water!"

My whole face was sore. I tried to speak and couldn't. I started to cry instead.

"It's no use making that noise, you brought it on yourself" Mum said, "You've been told before not to waste time when you've been sent on an errand." Of course Mum shouting only made things worse. I didn't know what had happened to me or why my face was hurting so much.

Some days later Mr Rodda, the owner of the tin-stream

works, called to find out how I was. Apparently he had learned from his employees that something had happened. I heard Mum saying, "There is no need for that, She should not have been poking her nose where she had no business. I don't want a man to lose his job because of her."

I had to wait until the Saturday when Mum and Dad went to the pictures before I was able to learn what had really happened. When Frank had looked through the crack he had seen a workman in the workshop chopping wood. He had told Frank to stop looking through. When he looked up again and saw me he thought it was the boy he had warned, so he threw what he still had in his hand, a 'dag', an axe. That was what had struck me. It had come right through the fence.

Luckily my eyes weren't affected, except for the swelling around them. My face and nose took some time to heal up. I was never sent to the doctor - we had to pay for medical treatment in those days.

# CHAPTER 7

When I returned to school I was called into the headmistress' study. It was explained to me that the Girls' County School (which was close to Camborne Railway Station) was requesting that six girls from Basset Road School who were doing well in spite of not having taken the eleven plus, or had taken the exam and only just missed out on passing it, be selected for an opportunity to train to be teachers. The Government was expecting a shortage of teachers in ten years' time, as people who might have applied were now involved in the services.

The teachers I remember at Basset Road were Miss Osborne, Miss Hendy and Miss Cowling. There was a lady who could not have been long out of college, as she always wore a green and white striped blazer. She taught us domestic science and nature study lessons. Her name was Miss Griffiths, and of course the music teacher was Miss James. I liked them all, including Miss Corfield, the Headmistress. If I could be as good as any of those I would do well.

The choice was to be left to the Headmistress. I entered her office trembling in fear, afraid I was in trouble because of my recent absence. I came out more than happy. She had decided I was to be one of the six!

I could hardly wait to get home to tell my parents. I was as clever as my brothers after all! And I could go to the County School!

Mum didn't want to listen. She said I could put such thoughts out of my head and I was only getting ideas above my station. Dad said they should hear me out, as it was something of an honour to be selected and he would need to have a good reason for not considering it. I then had to leave them to talk and Dad would tell me later what they had decided.

After I had got the young ones in to bed that evening, all the time hoping Mum would not be against my having this second chance, I was told by Dad that I could go for an interview to the Girls County School but to explain that I had never thought about becoming a teacher and would it be possible for me to train for something that would allow me to finish my schooling at fourteen, instead of sixteen, which was necessary if I trained for teaching, as I would be the first one to get a job and help the family finances by bringing wages home.

I was so ashamed. I could not tell the interviewers what Dad had said, so I told them I really wanted to be a nurse. They said they were sorry, as my headmistress had spoken well of me, and as they knew I already had a brother at Redruth Grammar School it was obvious we had some intelligence in the family.

Four of the six girls interviewed went on to go to the Girls County School. I don't know if they became teachers. The

Headmistress said she was disappointed at my decision and asked if I was sure. "After all," she said, "your parents will be proud of your achievements in years to come!" It was the nearest I had come to crying in public. If only she knew the truth!

I was doing well at school, and I had passed an art exam and won a place at the local art college, which was in Camborne in a large late 19th century building known as the Camborne School of Mines. It was used mainly for teaching mining students, with its own museum of metallurgy and geology specimens, and I was to attend on Saturday mornings between ten and twelve o'clock, so as not to interfere with my schoolwork.

I enjoyed the whole experience, including the mining museum part of the building with all the beautiful coloured specimens of stones and minerals. All went well for a few weeks. I was mainly interested in textile designs. But then Mum decided she needed to go shopping on Saturday mornings, and I was wanted at home to look after the youngsters.

It didn't help my disappointment either when a letter arrived from the art college stating that I had come second in the exam I'd taken there. In view of my high marks a place had been allocated for me and would I consider returning for the next term?

Mum would not permit me to go back. A short time after that she changed the arrangements again and I was sent back to work in the fields. That meant Mum could use the cash I earned to pay her bus fare into town on Saturday afternoons.

I'd lost out on other things too. I'd joined the Red Cross

Cadets at school. When the venue and time was changed to an early evening meeting, 5-6 pm, I had to give that up as there was no one to meet me when it finished. The boys had their own evening chores as well as homework to do and Dad was on shift work at East Pool and Agar Mine, so he would have only one week in three at home in the evenings. Mum would not allow me to come home on my own.

Aunt Evelyn was paying for Lizzie to have piano lessons with a Mr Apps, who lived at Roskear behind the church. Unfortunately he was sightless, so he required someone to accompany him to and from Aunty's cottage. She thought this was something I was quite capable of doing. She offered to pay me, or give me piano lessons at the same time as Lizzie.

I liked the idea of playing the piano, so said I would do it. I should have guessed it wouldn't suit Mum. After a couple of weeks I had to give it up. Piano playing wasn't for the likes of me, she said.

My sister Margaret reminds me of a time when we three girls were in bed together suffering from something contagious - we can't remember what. The doctor came and said Frances was clear and needn't stay with us. Mum was a bit put out about that because of having to pay for calling the doctor out in those days. She hoped we'd all get ill at the same time.

At this time my favourite subjects at school were to do with reading and writing. I was constantly asked to read to the class. Because I could never take money to school to pay for material for sewing lessons, I generally had to read poetry to the class instead. Mum always said "Your father can teach you how to sew all that you are likely to need.You've no need to pay for it".

I enjoyed drama lessons at school, and because I could remember poems and prose passages I was asked to try out for the next school play production, 'Dick Whittington'. I came home one day very happy because I had learnt a poem off by heart and recited it to Mum and Dad. It was called 'Drink to me only' and had nothing to do with plays.

Dad gave me a small book of poems written by a Reverend G A Studdert Kennedy, a Padre in the Army during the First World War. His nickname had been Woodbine Willie, on account of his generosity in issuing Woodbine cigarettes to the servicemen on their dispatch to the front lines during the fighting. The small poetry book, titled 'Rough Rhymes of a Padre', had also been issued to service personnel during World War II. The writing was similar to Rudyard Kipling's works, and that appealed to me (since returning to Cornwall I have been able to purchase three more of the same author's works. I still find them interesting). Dad had often got me to read some of the contents prior to this and always seemed pleased by the way I did it. But Mum said I shouldn't be learning such rubbish and told him off for encouraging me.

I got the part of Dick in the play and Dad made my costume, along with a very good black cat. On performance day the cat was supposed to follow me when I entered stage left. Unfortunately the prompt didn't throw it after me as instructed. Instead someone else who noticed it was still back stage opened a door and threw it so that it fell centre stage front. I rushed to collect it, ad-libbing about it having gone after a mouse etc. Luckily only the drama mistress realised what had happened. The prompt got a ticking off and I got praise for my quick thinking.

I've forgotten the following year's production, I think it was 'Beauty and the Beast', but I remember the last when I was selected to play Scrooge in Dickens 'A Christmas Carol'. My mother was very much against it, telling Dad to knock some sense into me and stop me involving myself in such nonsense. If not she threatened to go to the school and have words with the Headmistress.

Two of my female cousins lived at Falmouth, and one of them was very much involved in theatre; I had never seen her on stage, so it was not her influence that sparked my interest. I asked why it was all right for cousin Elsie to be involved in theatre, as Elsie's mum was my mum's sister and by all accounts nearly as strict as Mum was. "That was different" Mum said. "Elsie is old enough to work and be paid to entertain."

Dad said he couldn't see what harm an hour's play-acting at school could do, but the result was a lecture on the stupidity of what went on in theatres and how unlike real life it was. I thought about it and decided my best move was not to mention it any more at home. This left me with the problem of my costume.

Ironically it was the wielder of the axe at the tin stream who came to my rescue. He was an unusually short man and apparently a member of a dance band, playing at venues at weekends. As such he had an old dress suit which would be suitable for the early miserly scenes in Scrooge and a newer outfit for the later scene, and he was prepared to lend them to me. When the sewing mistress was approached, she provided material to make the nightshirt and cap for the dream scenes. I remember the kindness of those people who kitted me out, although I don't remember how it all came about.

In my final year we were taught Hungarian dancing, although a lot of the dances I remember had names such as Durham Reel, Circassian Circle and the Irish Washerwoman. Mum disagreed with this being a school lesson but as it had nothing to do with English dancing such as waltzing, foxtrot etc, she didn't fuss too much.

I had already been warned that I would never be permitted to go dancing. My parents view was that it wasn't natural for a boy and girl to hold each other that close all evening and then be able to say goodnight at their door afterwards! At thirteen, I had no idea what all that meant.

I loved the outfit for the Hungarian dancing. It consisted of a white organdie blouse, embroidered around the neckline down the front and on the sleeves with red and blue flowers, drawn in at the waist to imitate a frill. The skirt was black, flared, with three coloured bands, red, yellow and green, on lower half. We wore dark ankle socks and daps (soft canvas gym shoes) on our feet. Dad made those from a material known as Rexine. Coloured headscarves kept our hair in order.

We went to Truro for a large schools gathering, where we performed in front of officials and parents. We also visited many other schools and performed at local concerts, where the dancing was appreciated. Dad made my outfit and I was very proud to wear it.

Strangely, although Mum disliked my 'showing off nonsense' as she called it, Frank and Frederick, both now at Redruth Grammar School were able to take part in their school concerts. They were performing a sketch based on the song 'There's a Hole in my Bucket Dear Liza'. It was quite funny and they made a good job of it, but I could never understand why Mum didn't make any objections about them taking part in it.

I also failed to understand why, if Mum wanted me to have a good well-paid job when I left school, she blocked any opportunity for me to better the education I was getting. My brothers tried to teach me a little of the French they were learning at school, but that too was barred by Mum as 'useless' for me.

Although as children we understood very little about being at war, we did know what helping to do farm work and horticulture to help the war effort meant. Frank, Frederick and I were very involved in working on the land in our spare time. Climbing on the hay ricks and loading the wagon with sheaves was fun, as well as work. We often got fed by the farmers' wives, who would bring food and drink out to the fields to us.

One of my main memories is of riding home after that particular job on the back of a large shire horse and having to clutch desperately at the horse's mane to avoid sliding off of one side or the other. The shire's back was far too wide for my short legs.

The Government, we were told, was ordering landowners to double their production of crops and anything else which would feed the people. In the school holidays we would be out early mornings earning all we could. We were paid one shilling (5p) per day.

Italian prisoners of war were working on some farms, dressed in light brown dungarees with cream, yellow or orange patches. It was said that the majority of them were quiet, polite and good workers. They would arrive by lorry in the mornings, work until midday, sit together for their meal, work the afternoon and be taken back by lorry to where they were stationed in the late afternoon, and hardly a word was heard from them. They never spoke to us children.

# CHAPTER 8

The people were responding too to the 'Make do and Mend' appeals. The women were becoming quite ingenious at making something out of nothing. Necklaces and earrings were being fashioned out of milk-bottle tops, cup hooks and film spools, and even corks were adapted. With a few bits of ribbon or scraps of wool added it was surprising what some girls could achieve.

Dried milk tins were made into flower arrangements. Using very sharp cutters (Dad usually did this for me) and opening it from top to bottom on the opposite side to the seam, then laying it on its side and beginning half an inch from the bottom, we cut in toward the seam. By doing this every half an inch from edge to seam we ended up with lots of strips to which we attached crepe paper flowers. When I brought my family to Cornwall in the 1960s I saw one of these arrangements in the window of a house in Camborne.

Thinly-plaited Cellophane, similar to today's cling film but a little thicker, was made into belts and hair-bands. I never learned to do that; most of those would have been for the use of older girls who were permitted to grow their hair and do things to it.

Dad was kept busy turning old garments into new for people. He would carefully unpick the seams (he taught me to do this too), turn the material inside out and re-stitch it. Sometimes it would be like for like, eg a coat into a coat, but often it was making a smaller garment from a large one.

I was once sent to deliver a pair of trousers to an elderly lady who asked me to wait inside while she got the cash to pay for them, fourpence (10p). While I waited she went to a drawer, and imagine my terror when she withdrew a large carving knife and walked towards me. I quickly stepped to one side, but she walked right past me to the back wall and using the knife handle, she banged on the wall. A few minutes later her next-door neighbour appeared. It seemed the old lady only wanted to show off the trousers. I collected the payment and got out, still shaking!

On my way home from school one day I discovered a group of girls in a closed shop doorway shielding another girl who was painting the legs of one of the group with some sort of light brown dye to imitate stockings (which could no longer be purchased easily). For this she charged 2d per person, which was considered reasonable. The person being painted was expected to supply their own dye. I thought about the steady hand required to paint the straight seam down the back of the leg. Apparently this happened whenever there was a dance to be held in the local NAAFI (Navy, Army and Air Force Institute) in Camborne.

Frances talked about the American Army lorries loaded with soldiers which constantly passed when she was on her way to school. The men threw chewing gum, oranges and sometimes chocolate out to the local folk they passed. She said there was no way she would have picked any of it up though, as Mum would not allow her to have chewing gum. Frederick wasn't so choosey and he did catch an orange one day. He made sure he ate it before he got home.

Dad was also taking the opportunity to teach Frederick certain skills Frank and I had already learned. It was coming up to Christmas, Frederick recalls. Dad had asked him to come into the workshop and give him a hand. In there he had got a full-grown brown cockerel and he asked Frederick to hold it. He had not mentioned that he intended to kill it. Frederick says the bird didn't take too kindly to having a knife plunged into its neck. It gave one shriek and leapt from his hands, running behind the coal heap in the unlit corner. Dad gave my brother a good telling off, said he needed a cigarette and went back into the kitchen, followed by a sorrowful son. After the cigarette he handed Frederick a torch, telling him to go find the bird. When he found it, "dead as a dodo" as Frederick said, Dad instructed him to bring it out into the light, where he again tried to remove the head with a penknife that wasn't sharp enough for the job. Finally he used the chopper and decapitated the bird. It was then hung up over a bucket to drain any remaining blood. Dad said this was necessary to keep the meat white.

Next day Frederick got his first lesson in plucking and cleaning a chicken. We felt sorry for our brother, as he was only nine years old.

Four years later he started keeping a few chicken of his own, housing them in a run he made himself and kept on the unused gardens belonging to the empty cottages next door, to earn a bit of pocket money buying and selling. The earlier episode had taught him not to get sentimental over them.

Dad had also taught us all to clean, polish and refill his carbide miner's lamp. It was about three inches in diameter and four inches tall with a round reflector on the top. A small half-inch jet of flame came from a hole in the centre of the reflector when in use. The bottom two inches contained the carbide, a grey substance which was fine whilst dry but if it was allowed to get wet it sizzled and gave off a sulphur-like smell that was quite unpleasant.

Dad also liked his boots and helmet cleaned regularly. The boys were excellent at achieving a very high polish on them. I was always very proud of the way he looked compared with the other miners he walked to work with whenever I met him on the road.

Mum was proving herself helpful to a woman who lived in one of the cottages close to Aunt Evelyn. The lady was pregnant and had been told it could be twins. She was nervous of actually giving birth, yet she had already produced four children. I did not realise at that time that her youngest was already fourteen years old. She was thought to be old to start having children again after such a long gap.

She was not willing to go into the hospital. Mrs Ashton, the lady living next door to Mrs Bassett and fellow trustee at the church, was a midwife and presided over local births. She had advised Mrs Warne to go into hospital, but when her time came the twins were born at home, and one of them died. My mum said she would not help out at a birth again. it was unpleasant losing a child which might have been saved had it been born in the hospital

The boys borrowed a corner of one of Freddy Butler's fields, unknown to him, and started a growing plot of their own, thinking to earn some money for themselves. All went well until harvest time, when Freddy found out and confiscated what he decided was his property, so they lost everything.

I suspected Freddy knew all along, as he or his father-in-law walked the fields most evenings checking on livestock, gates etc. I couldn't believe they would have missed the boys' efforts. He must have decided he'd teach them a lesson by letting them do all the work of nursing the crops to fruition, then claiming the harvest. But all that was forgotten and it was a red-letter day for the boys when Freddy took delivery of a brand new iron-wheeled Fordson tractor, an event they didn't stop going on about for days. They hoped they might one day get to drive it.

Frank, Frederick and I were asked to go to a field not far from Camborne to do a job we'd not done before, weeding anemones. This was back-breaking work as the plantlets, much like baby carrot tops, were so tiny. After a couple of weeks Frank came home one day to say that the plantlets had all died! Apparently the land had once been used for landfill and some poisonous waste had been dumped there. The owner made a lot of fuss, claiming not to have been told about it when he bought the field, but we never learned the outcome.

One day during the school summer holiday when the weather was warm and we didn't have to go to work Frank suggested that he, Frederick and I should go to Portreath. After paddling about in the surf (none of us could swim), we decided it was time to go home, but just as we got to the entrance who should appear on his bicycle but Dad. We went back to our spot on the beach and Dad produced some food from his haversack. We were all hungry, so we enjoyed a sandwich and Cornish 'heava cake' before leaving for home. Apparently he had arrived home from work and was annoyed with mum for letting us go off with no food or drink.

Another incident happened during those holidays and I've been reminded of it by a friend, Jack Andrews. He lived in the same group of four cottages as Aunt Evelyn. Apparently when he went for milk one afternoon he discovered several boys, my brothers and the three Warne boys among them, in the milking barn. Freddy Butler must have been having a boyish half an hour. He had all the boys lined up with their mouths open and was squirting the milk straight from the cows' teats into the open mouths! (As an adult Jack, after many years working on the sea front and the Gyllandune Gardens at Falmouth, became Radio Cornwall's Gardening Expert. He related that story over the air one evening.)

Also during these holidays, one of the Catteral brothers gave Frederick permission to help himself to an apple from a tree in the orchard. Someone told Dad my brother had been scrumping. Fred was lucky, as Dad believed his story so no punishment ensued. Frank wasn't as fortunate. He was in an orchard with three other boys intent on getting fruit without permission. He was lookout, but failed to see the owner approaching. The other boys scarpered and the owner caught Frank and marched him home, but Dad was at work. The owner went off in a huff, leaving Frank to worry for days, expecting a punishment that never materialised.

Dad had been asked to tar the roof of a garage for someone. He passed the job on to Frederick, instructing him to buy the tar, use an old brush of Mum's and claim for a new one when he made out the invoice. Unfortunately the customer asked for the new brush to be given to him. Bang went Frederick's profit, as he then had to purchase a new one for the garage owner. He did take the precaution of dipping it in the tar to make it appear used before handing it over.

One afternoon Frank was left to look after the farm when a man came with a heifer expecting to use the services of Freddy's young bull. Frank got the bull out and it went mad at seeing the heifer. With the help of the visiting farmer all went well, until Frank tried to return the bull to the barn. It refused to go back in. Finally Frank had to leave it to calm down, but he had to remain in the yard until the family returned after dark to warn them the bull was loose.

# CHAPTER 9

By this time the Government was trying new ideas for supplying food. Whale meat was one, but according to the wireless it wasn't liked, neither was tuna fish. There was a national wholemeal loaf, which was very dry, but the change from the awful grey loaf that the white bread had become because of the additives used to cut down on white flour was appreciated.

Dried eggs were supplied. It was a yellow powder and four ounces was equivalent to nine eggs. We used that a lot at home. Other dried food was meat, milk, potatoes and cabbage.

It was about this time that I was asked to go and sit with a little girl, the daughter of Mrs Saundry, a friend of Mum's, while the parents went out for the evening. It was too late for me to go home when they returned and it had been agreed I stayed the night.

Next morning I was asked what I would like for my breakfast. I suggested anything that wouldn't be too much trouble or the same as the family were having. I was told they were having poached egg on toast. I had no idea what it was, but as we older ones at home didn't have fresh eggs often it sounded good. I enjoyed it very much, and it was certainly something I'd learn how to cook given the opportunity.

A canning factory had been opened at Treswithian outside Camborne to dry the food, although I was told at school that it was purpose-built for supplying food and milk to the troops, who were desperate for supplies.

Sausages became a comedian's joke on the radio. They were called 'Britain's secret weapon!' or 'Breadcrumbs in battledress!' Comical posters of them were on lots of placards, along with 'Careless talk costs lives' 'Dig for victory', etc. It didn't help people's morale that posters appeared on hoardings of mouth-watering luxury foods captioned 'Not till after the war' or 'On Active Service'.

The 'Dig for Victory' leaflet issued by the Ministry of Agriculture encouraged folk to grow for all the seasons. It claimed that by digging well and planting wisely you could have fresh vegetables every week of the year, including winter when normal supplies were scarce. It gave instructions when to carry out each operation, what to plant and when harvest could be expected.

The Ministry of Food issued a special leaflet on 'Food and the health of your child'. It gave advice on what foods were required to build the various parts of a child's body and how much food was needed to build bones, muscle and teeth. This was backed up by the Government's scheme to give free milk in school. A leaflet on fuel saving in the kitchen was also issued, together with wartime cookery recipes in the National Food Campaign exhibition.

We were instructed to place all cardboard and waste paper to one side, not in the dustbins. Other leaflets advised about war on disease. Stick-on soles came into being and were supposed to save on leather. Dad got hold of some old rubber tyres which he used to repair our shoes. We were all pleased to have him home with us, and the boys said that after going around with cardboard in their shoes for months it was nice to have dry feet once more.

My brother Frederick told everyone Dad was multi-talented, and as long as he had the materials he could turn his hand to anything. He cut our hair and being something of a tailor, having been taught by a qualified seamstress while in her care as a youth, he made us clothes. Although Frederick wasn't so pleased with a pair of trousers Dad made for him from an old coat. They were bright pink! Frederick refused to wear them. Dad also knitted small garments for the youngest boys. He made a doll and dressed it as a soldier for Margaret.

Frances noted that some people remarked that the boys sometimes did look as if Dad had put a basin on their head and cut around it. We girls always had our hair kept short – Mum wouldn't have it left to grow in case of nits. Frances did have an attack of the nasty creatures and was sent home from school by the nit nurse. Mum wasn't there at the time, so Dad read the note and promptly washed Frances' hair in paraffin. It did kill the nits. Normally we used a black soap called Durbac. I had no trouble with them thankfully.

Frederick had difficulty at school. Being mad on sports he played rugby for the Cornwall under-fifteens, but he lacked a strip and had no money to buy it. The master found him an old jersey and a pair of football boots in the lost property box, but it wasn't enough, and he wasn't permitted to play visiting teams in a rubbish strip. It was the same when he was picked to play for the county cricket team. Apparently he was considered a good player, but without the correct gear he got nowhere.

He did once gain, on a very wet day. The master found him a navy blue gabardine mackintosh and a pair of wellington boots. Frederick claimed they were a bit big, but they kept him warm and dry for months.

Dad was never pleased with Frederick's academic report. He always claimed too much effort was placed on other things, such as sport.

It was about this time that a Lady Macrobert of Dounside gave a cheque for £20,000 for an aeroplane to carry on the work of her sons who had been killed on active service. Later she repeated it, and it started a savings movement called the Spitfire Fund, after the famous fighter plane. There were posters saying, 'Lend to defend the right to be free', 'War weapons week', 'Salute the Soldier Week'. The one we children liked best was 'Wings for Victory Week'.

All the towns and villages would compete to see who could raise the most savings, and a target board was set up in Camborne. Everyone kept an eye on how the fund was growing. A horrible insect called a squander bug appeared on posters, warning about spending more than you needed. Another poster designed by a fourteen-year-old girl depicted Hitler, the number one enemy, with his face covered so he could not see the coffin at his feet. It said, 'Every penny saved is a nail in Hitler's coffin'.

One day at school, well into the morning, I was sent to the headmistress' study. I met Pat, an evacuee from a house also at Roscroggan, on the way, as she too had been sent for. I knocked quietly on the door and on being told 'come in' we entered. Miss Corfield was looking very serious. She informed us in a gentle voice that there had been bomb damage at Roscroggan and we were to go home at once in case we could be of any help.

We needed no second bidding. We grabbed our coats from the pegs in the cloakroom and ran. Normally we'd have been stopped and told not to. We didn't slow down until a stitch in the side forced me to, and Pat was out of breath. A few knee-bends and we were on our way again, walking this time until we reached the top of the hill where we could see the roofs of both our houses.

Then we noticed the smoke and flames. At the bottom of the hill on the right the old white chapel, which had stood there firmly in the morning, was burning fiercely. A few yards further away on the left there was also a fire. A coppice of small trees down the lane where cousin Lizzie and me had gone flower picking when I first arrived at Roscroggan had something large and made of metal burning in it.

A policeman came toward us, asking why we weren't in school. When I explained he said, "You need not concern yourselves, no houses have been damaged." Pat said "Oh that's good" and disappeared up the lane to her own home. The boys arrived soon after I got indoors; they too had been sent home from school.

Mum said we could all go to the farms and see what work was required. The boys raced upstairs to change out of uniforms and into working gear, but as they slipped out of the house they shouted back that they were going to see the fire. I didn't find it so easy to escape, and Mum very soon found jobs for me to do.

When the news finally leaked out, it transpired that the aircraft was a Bristol Beaufort Fighter Bomber, a Ferry Flight No 1 Unit. It had left Portreath Aerodrome with a crew of four and somehow failed to reach the required height. The pilot must have seen the white chapel and nearby Turner's Bungalow and taken a chance on the chapel not being in use on a weekday, he swerved to avoid the bungalow. All four men in the plane were killed. The chapel was in use only as a store-house for bales of jute, and the resultant fire from the wingtip caught the rooftop on its way down, causing no local injuries.

I have often wondered what we could have done had our houses been hit by bombs. We were only children. Who would have been responsible for us when we arrived home from school had something happened to our parents?

Some of the local women, Mum included, went off in a group that evening to see what damage had been done. I don't know what they found as I was left in charge of the house and told to 'mind my own business' when I asked on her return. I was then sent off to bed before Dad came home from work after late shift.

As I write this a memorial plaque to these men has been placed where the White Chapel once stood. I believe the chapel may have been built of cob, and apart from the jute inside, that was why it burned so readily. Sadly the small car park opened opposite for visitors to the memorial has had to be blocked off due to the thoughtless use of it by people disposing of scrap cars and household rubbish.

By this time the boys and I had all learned to deliver milk. I loved to drive out the farm's pony and trap. Very few people could drive cars, so other than horse and carts there was very little traffic on the road and driving the trap for me was easy.

Sometimes when the deliveries were finished I'd get to take the pony to another of the fields to give him fresh pasture to feed on. I took advantage of every opportunity to ride. On the road I felt very grown up, and although I had no saddle I sat up straight, behaving as well as I thought I should. In the fields I'd ride with less inhibition, galloping around and behaving like the schoolgirl I really was.

I don't know what I thought I looked like. My clothes were disgraceful. I had old trousers of Dads, a jersey with holes in that had belonged to one of the boys and wellington boots for all the field work.

Frederick used to take a full milk churn on a trolley out to the main road before going to school. It was collected later by the Milk Marketing Board lorry and an empty churn left in its place, which Frederick would bring back to the farm after school. Then he'd deliver milk to several cottages nearby. For this he had a large churn on a four-wheeled trolley and two measures, one pint and one quart. He'd measure the milk into the customers' own jugs at their door. He was paid a shilling a week and Mum allowed him to keep tuppence. This arrangement ended when the Milk Marketing Board decided that milk had to be pasteurised and bottled before it could be sold to customers.

He then got a job delivering meat orders for Butcher Williams. One day he had one order left in the basket when he met a school friend who lived next door to the lady whose order it was, and the friend offered to deliver it for him. Fred willingly handed it over. He wasn't to know the friend would stop off for a game of football on his way home, shoving the packet of meat wrapped up in white paper into his coat pocket. The customer protested at the state of her order, and that was the end of that job.

One day while on school holiday, after returning from my paper round in the morning, I'd gone to the lavatory when I heard a dreadful commotion outside. I was afraid to venture out, until at last all I could hear was a cow bellowing. Finally I plucked up the courage. On emerging I discovered that the noise was coming from a hole in the waste ground of a walled area opposite.

I raced down to the farm and told Enid, and the men came with a tractor and ropes. A man was lowered into the hole, which was in fact an uncapped mine shaft, to fasten a rope under the cow's belly and another around its legs. After what seemed hours the cow was hauled up out of the shaft, the man following it. After a feed the animal was none the worse for its escapade. Apparently it had happened before and was expected to do so again.

When I queried why such dangerous shafts still remained

uncovered, Enid said the mines were extinct and so old that nobody knew who the original owners were. Capping them would be prohibitive, and for the odd occurrence such as had just happened it would not be worth the expense.

On the left of the unmade lane leading up to the tall chimney stacks there was a large area of common land called the Burrows. It was covered in gorse, furze (ferns) and blackberry bramble. Frank used it as a short cut, cycling through it at speed every day. There were several uncapped shafts on it, of which we had no knowledge until Enid told me to warn the boys. I don't think it stopped Frank or any of the village boys. Meanwhile Freddy would re-fence the edge of the field above the shaft and trust his cows stayed away from the hedge they'd fallen through.

On the right of the same lane was an orchard with cherry trees that overhung the fence. Frances loved picking them when they were ripe. "Very sweet" she reckoned, although I cannot remember picking them.

# CHAPTER 10

One day when I was coming home from shopping with Mum, we saw Dad coming toward us. As he got closer I saw that his face and hands were covered with blood. Mum screamed at him "Fred what have you done?" When he reached us he would have fallen if we hadn't got the pram for him to lean on.

It transpired that a kibble (a square four-wheeled truck that conveyed the ore along rails underground) had blown up when full. Dad had been at the back of it and had taken some of the blast. He was left to walk the three miles home with no escort or treatment!

My earlier first-aid teaching with the Red Cross came in useful once we reached home. On removing his top clothing we found Dad's chest was pitted with flakes of rusted iron, torn skin and congealed blood. It took me an hour to clean his wounds and plaster him with St James's Balm.

He had been ordered to visit the doctor's as soon as possible and he went the next day. Thankfully it appeared nothing had penetrated too far in past the first layer of skin, and my prompt cleaning had been satisfactory enough to prevent any infection setting in. It had not cost him anything - Mum was pleased when he broke that news. Although things were different when he informed us that he had been advised to try and get work other than down the mine, outdoor work if possible.

Camborne had two picture houses. The entrance to the Scala was next door to the town clock. The exit, used also by the skating rink downstairs, was around the corner. The other was the King's Cinema opposite the large Post Office building and only a few steps away from the Camborne Methodist Church, which was well attended with large congregations in those days.

During the early days of the war the picture houses had been closed. Large notices had been posted outside each, stating 'Closed for the Duration'. As children we could not have gone to see films anyway.

One day Frederick, with a little money in his pocket, set off, catching the bus that ran on two days per week only for visitors to Tehidy Sanatorium (it would pick up passengers on its way back to Camborne), intending to go to the Scala. He was under age, so the cashier wouldn't allow him in in spite of his claiming his older sister was inside. When he met a boy who told him how to get in around the back he took the advice. But the usherette was wise to it, and he soon found himself out on the street again.

I do remember going to the Odeon at Falmouth as a seven-year-old. They had a Mickey Mouse club for children up to the age of ten. I had a card that was stamped with a star each time I attended. I don't recall how I got there or who I went with, but when I mentioned it at Roscroggan Mum said I was too old now and there was no Odeon Cinema in Camborne, and that I had been living at Penryn at the time.

The boys got to do things like going camping in Tehidy woods, or fishing for minnows, sticklebacks and tadpoles in a pond on the way to Camborne. I never managed anything like that, but I did on one occasion arrange a concert in the garden of another Basset Road School girl who lived at the top of the hill near to Mrs Bassett. Frederick began making us a stage, but somehow it was never finished. I do remember singing a song called 'My little grey home in the west' and that we charged a penny entrance to neighbours.

One day during another school summer holiday, Frank and Frederick were bored, and went down to the farm looking for something to do. None of the owners seemed to be about. They spotted one of the farm's white chicken and chased it around and around until it collapsed. Frederick put it in one of the chicken houses, but unfortunately it died. Someone must have seen them, because Freddie Butler came to the house telling mum that it had been one of his best layers. The boys told me it cost them half a crown (12.5p) and a lot of grief.

At the back and side of our row of cottages were fields, all belonging to the farm. They were all named, for example Chute field, Corn Field, Square Field and Hay Field. Right up behind the cottage was Long Field, where Freddy often put the cows.

One day David had been coming across the field when a cow named June chased him. He told Frederick he cleared the five-barred gate with inches to spare just in time to escape being gored. Apparently David had helped to separate the cows from the calves in the farmyard prior to putting them out to grass and June must have remembered him. We often heard the cows calling for their calves after they'd been parted. It always made me sad.

Cornish women were known for being hard working, especially the farmers' wives, and now the women whose husbands were serving their country were having an extremely rough time. Not only were they replacing the men in several labouring occupations they would not have expected to become involved in, they were struggling to keep things on an even keel at home. With all the shortages, meals and the planning of them became a constant battle.

More and more of them turned their hands to gardening, and flower-beds became vegetable plots. The smell of potato and mixed vegetable peelings being boiled up for meals for poultry became an easily recognised sign of the women raising chickens when I delivered the papers.

It was also a cheap way of obtaining more than the standard one egg per ration book allowed by the Government. There was the knowledge too that if by chance 'folk had more eggs than they required, they could be sold at farmers' markets, earning a little extra pocket money.

Furniture wasn't rationed but the sale of it was controlled, so it was difficult to buy. Couples who were planning their wedding or preparing their future homes at the time were allocated 60 coupons. This was considered ample until the number was cut to 30, which proved only enough to buy a table, chairs, a bed and wardrobe. Plain white was all there was in new crockery. Cutlery was made of an easily-broken alloy. Saucepans were in short supply, so Mum was glad she had saved her iron ones.

I remember at this time at school we were taught to make string bags. These were made in the same way as fishing nets, but with string, using a flat wooden needle about one inch wide with a barb, like hook. They were considered very useful because they would stretch to accommodate a fair bit of shopping, and they well replaced the shopping bags that could no longer be purchased, apart from when it rained!

One afternoon I had been sent to Tuckingmill with one of the young children in the pushchair, to buy potatoes and bread. On the return journey Jean from next door caught us up. For some reason she was in an aggravating mood, and as we reached the narrow bridge over the tailing lake she pushed past me, reached down and tipped my bag of shopping into the red lake below us.

My mother must have been watching for me from the bedroom window, for she came out shouting for me to hurry up. Jean carried on into her own house as though nothing had happened. When mum realised I'd got no groceries she was angry. I was charged with having upset Jean and she went next door to talk to Mrs Mankee, who gave her the money to replace the lost goods.

Frank got sent off to the shop and I had to do his chores that evening as well as my own. This meant fetching four buckets of water and chopping sticks for fire lighting next day. My regular jobs were helping prepare tea, washing up tea dishes, getting the younger ones ready for bed and checking school clothes. I don't ever recall having homework from school.

On Saturdays the routine was slightly changed. Mum and Dad went to the pictures at Camborne. The boys also had to fill the coal bucket with 'churks', a coke-like substance left after the gas had been removed from coal, and clean all the shoes. My own jobs were added to by peeling vegetables for next day and ironing. I had also to supervise children washing themselves and make sure everyone except me was in bed before my parents arrived home, and woe betide me if they weren't. Sometimes the boys stayed out playing until it was too late to get everything done, and I would try to finish it for them, anything to avoid Mum's anger!

On days when I delivered the papers in the morning I often had to go to the tip and collect churks in the afternoon. The tip was behind the two large 150ft chimney stacks up the lane at Tolvaddon, about a ten-minute walk away. Dad had made a four-wheeled dandy for this purpose. It was big enough to carry four half-hundred weight sacks full of churks. Mum preferred using this in the Cornish Range, as it gave out more heat than some of the slatey coal we were getting and of course it was free for the collecting. This was the sort of advice being given by the Ministry of Food in their fuel-saving leaflet, so we who were old enough to go out collecting churks felt we were also helping the war effort.

One fine sunny afternoon I had taken David with me on this errand, as he loved riding in the dandy on the outward journey. He lived only for being out in the fresh air and studying anything to do with nature. We had almost filled the sacks when a large crow flew down quite close to us. It was in no way bothered at our movements, but just kept hopping around, and finally stood watching us from the shelter of our dandy. David became quite excited. "Ooh look!" He said, "that crow thinks it's a pigeon, it walks with its toes facing in." For a not-quite-seven year old I thought he was clever to notice that.

Incidentally I had discovered that the stacks were arsenic flues. Beneath them were several sheds or 'houses' where the men, suitably attired in white, including masks and head coverings, on certain days spent time scraping this poisonous white powder from the walls. For several years prior to this there had been many businesses in this lethal trade in Cornwall. Cattle and people were sadly killed by land and water pollution. Thankfully it has now finished entirely.

One day on my way to school I'd met up with two friends, Pat and John, evacuees from London. A brother and sister, they'd been lucky enough to get in with the same family. Although they were twins and the same age as me they were much older in their ways. They had already learned to smoke and seemed always to have pocket money, which John often spent on cigarettes. My parents smoked, but I had no idea how to.

This particular morning John turned up with a small green paper packet containing five Woodbine cigarettes. It had cost him twopence halfpenny (1.05p). Pat took one and insisted I tried, and I did, and choked on it. I was being heartily thumped on the back when the Headmistress, Miss Corfield, drove by in her car. She stopped and asked if I was all right, and Pat said I'd swallowed something.

In school assembly Miss Corfield announced that it had come to her notice that pupils had been seen smoking in a public place. She hoped this wasn't so, but she didn't ask for the culprit to own up. I avoided her eyes as much as possible from then on.

My brothers weren't so lucky. Dad had discovered that Frank had been trying to smoke. One day after school he called both boys into his bedroom and gave each of them a cigarette, saying "smoke it". Frederick had never tried before and hated it immediately. Frank carried on until Dad took the cigarettes away.

They found out later that although Dad usually smoked a small mild brand himself, he'd actually bought the very strong Capstan Extra, hoping to teach the boys a lesson. Frederick never did take up the habit. I never let on that I'd tried, not wanting one of Dad's 'lessons'.

# CHAPTER 11

Frances remembers Dad's talents for making things. She reminds me of the time he made sister Margaret a doll's pram and herself a trike. Every bit of each item was made of wood, but she didn't have her trike long as I sat on it and broke it.

Which reminds me of an earlier episode with Frank. It was his birthday three days after my own, and I had received a china doll. Within hours Frank had smashed its head in, simply because he thought he should have got presents at the same time as me! We were about five or six. Such is the cruelty of children!

One day some men delivered an Anderson Air Raid Protection Shelter, which was left for Dad and the boys to erect. It was made of galvanised iron and took up half of our small garden, and they spent hours assembling it. It left very little room for the potatoes and other vegetables Dad grew.

We had a few roses, and Frances remembers collecting horse manure after the coal deliveryman had been through with his horse and cart. She would often bring in lumps of coal that had been dropped off the straight-sided cart, but not before she had spat on it and thrown it over her shoulder as a way of encouraging good luck.

None of the family remembers making use of the shelter during an air raid, and it was always half filled with muddy water. Some say they were pushed in under the double bed in the front room, under the kitchen table or just crouching down indoors. I recall being under the stairs at one time.

The bombers, when they came, had such a different droning sound to the engines from our own planes that we did get a fair warning. The majority of the raids were directed at Falmouth Docks, where a great deal of damage was inflicted over the years.

Aunt Evelyn had a different make of shelter, a Morrison Shelter. It consisted of a cage-like structure that went over a large kitchen table. Frances, who was often over there playing with our cousin Percy, got put into it one day with him.

Of course we all carried our gas masks everywhere. Issued in 1938 anticipating the war, I remember being fitted for one but I don't think I ever put it on again except for practice.

Today the smell of rubber close by reminds me of the claustrophobic feeling I experienced with mine on my face. David and Frances, being young, had what was termed a 'Mickey Mouse mask'. It was coloured red and blue, while adult masks were grey and black. Babies were placed in a cradle-like structure, laid down, and clipped in.

The masks were issued in square, sturdy cardboard boxes and Dad made Rexine covers for ours, protecting them from rain. Soon other people saw the advantages and started ordering them. I delivered dozens of them; he charged 4d (2p) each.

David hated school. He was a pupil at Roskear and when

Mum found out that he had been 'minchin' (playing truant), Frank and I were ordered to walk him to school between us before going to our own schools. We believed this worked for a time until we discovered he was waiting until we left him and off he would scamper. We then started taking him right inside the school door, but he still managed to escape.

He was a tough-looking little boy with very short fair hair that didn't grow very quickly. Because of this his head appeared more square than round. Workmen we passed on the way to school nicknamed him Mussolini, although not many of us children knew who they were likening him to at that time. On his way home one day, David threw all his books in the river and ran away. He returned late in the evening. He never did lose his love of the outdoors.

When East Pool and Agar Mine closed down, Dad applied for work at other mines. Finally he got taken on at Geevor Mine, located down west at St Just. This put more financial strain on him because he then had two homes to keep going, ours and the lodgings. I'm not sure how long he remained there, but it soon proved too much.

Frederick had qualified for a green card, allowing him to work in the school holidays. After doing all sorts of fieldwork for local farmers he was employed part-time by a family named Purcel. They were digging up spent daffodil bulbs, picking anemones, weeding new growths and doing a variety of jobs connected with horticulture. The produce was destined for the London market. The family were so pleased with the way

Frederick worked that they raised his wages to the same as the men who worked for them. This doubled his income so, as he was expected to do the same as the rest of us and hand over his unopened wage packet, Mum was also pleased with him and gave him a half a crown (two shillings and sixpence or 12.5p) back. He saved until he had £1, buying himself a second-hand bicycle, which he smartened up a bit to make himself independent for transport.

Although our parents never showed any interest in Frederick's sporting prowess, Mum did encourage him in his singing in the school choir. The highlight of the year was to sing as part of a two-thousand-strong choir in Truro Cathedral to be broadcast on the BBC. Mum listened to it on the radio and claimed she could pick his voice out above all the others! His talent ended when his voice broke.

Frederick managed to get Dad a job on the Purcels' farm. Mrs Purcel later told him that Dad was an excellent worker.

There was an addition to the family when I was thirteen. Another baby sister! She was named Elizabeth Anne. As this meant extra help needed at home, I had to give up another of the pastimes I enjoyed,

I had been going to the Tehidy hospital occasionally as part of my Red Cross Cadet training. This involved me in helping to serve afternoon tea to bedridden patients, rolling bandages and generally helping out where needed. I was also allowed to assist in caring for a little girl named Tina. I don't know what was specifically wrong with her but she was fed a diet solely of dried banana. She was four years old.

Frederick and David did their best gathering churks to save mum buying coal. One afternoon a lady met them on their way to the tip. When she asked where they were going Frederick said, 'to pick churks'. The lady must have misheard his reply, for she said she hoped it was a good film. Frederick wondered what she imagined they would be doing taking a large bucket and garden spade to the pictures!

# CHAPTER 12

I was almost 14, very busy and looking forward to changing my way of life again. I had been working extremely hard on the land and had even had a go at the heavy horse and plough, planting potatoes. I was fairly strong but not being very big, the job was too hard on my arms. I fancied I'd have liked a permanent farming life. Looking after the animals and growing plants appealed to me, but this didn't go down well at home. I think my Mum wanted me to get a well-paid job, and farming wasn't on the agenda. Neither was going into service, because she realised that if I went away to work she wouldn't get any wages for me at home.

I asked about learning to become a nurse, and Dad wrote a letter to the Redruth Hospital requesting details. I was called for an interview, and Mum decided to accompany me.

Because of my lack of County School education the Matron stipulated I would need to go to the Camborne/Redruth Technical College for two years or stay on at my present school and attend the College in the evenings. Mum explained the need for me to bring wages into the home. The Matron didn't think

I would be sufficiently dedicated to the caring side of nursing, and that was the end of that interview.

I still had some weeks to go at school. One of my friends was having a party for her 14th birthday. Knowing I was soon to be 14 myself, she invited me to the party. At that time I had done something to make Mum angry with me, and I was banned from going outside the house except for school and field work for two weeks. This was not an unusual occurrence, though I very seldom knew what I had done to earn my detention. I begged Joan to get her Mum to send me an official invitation. Joan had told me she was sending out several anyway, and that way Mum would have to reply and explain why I couldn't attend.

Joan's family thought leaving school and going out to work was a time to celebrate. They were even expecting her brother in the Army to be home on embarkation leave, another reason for a celebration. When the letter arrived Mum, of course, said no.

Dad was on day shift at the mine, and when he came home he asked what I had done to be disciplined. Whatever it was he didn't consider it warranted Mum being so strict. To save another argument he agreed I could go to the party, but only if Frank could go with me.

Joan was quite pleased to hear about Frank; she was keen on him, but because he was at the grammar school she thought he would be too grand for her. Her father said he would be fetching us in his car and bringing us home, so my parents need have no worries we would be out on our own after dark. I got my first kiss from a boy that afternoon, playing Postman's Knock. It didn't mean much - we were both too shy and didn't know what we were supposed to do! We hadn't met before either.

The tea her mum laid on was delicious. In spite of the war and rationing she had somehow managed to make several pastry savouries, sandwiches with fillings I'd never tasted before and an assortment of fancy buns. There was also a lovely birthday cake with 14 candles on, which Joan did manage to blow out all at once.

Joan was given a more grown-up outfit of clothes and shoes, to celebrate discarding the school uniform when leaving school the forthcoming Easter. But the treat her Dad had decided to surprise her with was a trip to the Gem Cinema at Redruth, taking anyone she liked to invite with her. She invited Frank and me and three other girls from school plus a couple of their brothers.

Her brother had written to say he would not arrive in time for tea but hoped to make it on the train early evening. He was also bringing a mate with him. Frank decided he wouldn't come to the cinema as he had homework to do, and Joan's dad dropped him off on the way to Redruth. I wondered if I should have gone home too, but he promised he'd tell Mum and Dad I was especially invited and I would be transported home later.

That was a really special day for me. I didn't have birthday parties because Frank, baby brother Philip and I had birthdays in February and David's was in early March. Mum couldn't afford to have one party in February and then another in March, so Frank and I had always to wait until March.

Two days later I arrived home after doing my paper round to be given no tea, told to go into the front bedroom and wait for my dad to come home from work. I was used to Mum keeping me in the house if she thought I'd misbehaved or disobeyed her in some way. Wondering what I had done this time, I tried to catch Frank's attention as he went quietly upstairs. He too seemed sad and shook his head at me, which told me nothing.

I heard dad arrive and a few minutes later he came in carrying the family Bible, shutting the door behind him.

"Where were you on Friday evening?" he said.

"At Joan's birthday party" I answered.

"I want the truth," he said, opening the Bible. "Your mother tells me you've lied to us and to make matters worse you have included Frank in your lies."

I was angry. I had seen how kindly Joan's parents had treated her – why should I be treated so differently? I was being punished for something I didn't know I'd done, again! Whatever it was they could at least be honest about it.

I stood up, and although I was afraid I looked my dad straight in the eye. "Why doesn't Mum tell me what I've supposed to have done?" I said. "I've not been allowed any tea, and you are telling me I've lied. Well tell me what is it I've lied about."

My father glared at me before saying "I've asked you for the truth. If I explain to you what I've been told will you promise to tell the truth?"

I had no qualms about answering him, as I'd had ample time sitting there on my own to think what I could possibly have done recently and there was nothing. He held the Bible open toward me. I put my hand on it.

"I promise" I said.

"It seems that a certain lady called here today and told your mother that you and a gang of other girls were with soldiers in the picture house at Redruth on Friday evening."

I tried to think who the lady could have been, but I couldn't even remember the name of the film now, and I was so angry that Mum couldn't even ask me in a proper manner. With the exception of the postman's knock game I explained to Dad exactly what had taken place on the previous Friday, and I suggested he check with my friend Joan's family for confirmation. He said he'd take my word for it, but he didn't know if Mum would.

Dad was right, but what made it worse was her belief that Frank was also to be doubted. My mother didn't speak to me for days except to call me Daddy's pet, when Dad wasn't around to hear her. I finally managed to ask the neighbour if she had seen anyone calling at our house on the day in question. She had, and mentioned the name of a neighbour to the farm situated across the valley. This lady owned a donkey and shay. We were used to seeing her about, but why she should be interested in me I had no idea. She wasn't one of my newspaper customers, but whatever the reason she had succeeded in causing trouble for me.

It always hurt that Mum never asked when she wanted to know something or apologised for her treatment of me. Even if she found out she was wrong, somehow she didn't want to believe it. Of course she never checked on anything. It was much easier to dish out the punishment first.

We had visits from relatives of Dad. They were his stepsister, Elsie, Elsie's husband Richard and their five children. They lived at Kehelland, just outside Camborne, but we never went to visit them. Some of their children were also attending Basset Road School, but we hadn't met before.

My mother didn't care for Dad's stepsister. She found out that Aunty Elsie had somehow managed to stop having any more children after the fifth (my mother always claimed she wanted the large family she'd got). I was warned to have nothing to do with them and not to encourage them to visit. No explanation was given to me.

# CHAPTER 13

How it came about I'm not sure, but when I finally left school I was sent to the canning factory. Mum had heard about it somewhere. I didn't know anything about factory work and I didn't like the sound of it, but as it was a good two and a half miles away I would at least get fresh air walking there and back each day, and I had managed to please Mum with the amount of wages I'd get.

The first few days weren't too strenuous, but there was no way I could go into the fields as well in the evenings. I was too tired. As it was I did the boys' chores so that they could help the war effort.

Three months into the job, and for the first time my femininity let me down. I suffered dreadful stomach cramps. Because I was at work I was sent to see the first aid nurse at the factory, who was surprised I had not been prepared by my mother for this natural happening. Nurse reported that I was in too much pain to be allowed to continue lifting the twenty-eight pound tins of dried food, and sent me home.

After Mum's warning that I could not expect days off every

month and I had better get used to working life whilst not feeling well, I was given Dad's bicycle to return to the factory next day. Mum decided that if I didn't have to walk I should be better able to perform my duties when I got there. The forewoman sent for the nurse and after a consultation they sent me home again, this time with a note saying I was not fit for that type of work. End of job!

Two weeks later I was found a job in a fish-and-chip café as a waitress, and trained to serve in the take-away shop. The shop was at the top end of Trelowarren Street in Camborne and my hours were 8am-2pm. I then got a break until 4pm, when I was on duty again until 9pm. With the two-mile walk there and back each day, because Mum insisted I went home in between each session as well, the day seemed endless.

I did get my tea supplied. One Monday I was given soused mackerel and chips. The fish were soaked in vinegar overnight then baked in the oven. I had never tasted this before but as I liked fish I enjoyed it, until I was given it every day for two weeks!

Three months after starting I thought I was doing well, but I arrived one morning to find that unusually, the owner had got there before me. She informed me my services were no longer required. When I asked why, I was shown a sink dirty with bits of raw fish. I was told that if the fish-man-cutter was unable, due to having to leave early at night occasionally, to clean it before leaving then it was my responsibility to clean it for him.

I pointed out that no one had told me this before - the man said he had mentioned it but I had ignored him. This was untrue, but as he had been with the firm for many years I stood no chance. In those days you could be sacked at a minute's notice so I was soon walking back home, crying all the way. What trouble I would be in when I got there I dreaded to think.

Although I consoled myself somewhat with thoughts that it would not have been hygienic for me to have done such a dirty, smelly job whilst being employed as a waitress, I knew I should receive no sympathy from Mum. I had been sacked again, and I'd only been working for six months altogether.

As I suspected, my name was mud at home. For the next three or four days everyone was told about my inability to hold down a job. But Aunt Evelyn made her feelings known, and she didn't believe it was my fault. She said "Why don't you let her go to the Labour Exchange? They will ask her questions and get her to fill in a form and then find her something she is cut out for."

Mum said, "She hasn't been able to keep either of the two jobs she's been given so far so she wouldn't know what to tell them at the Labour Exchange. She'll have to wait until I can go with her". Aunty offered to take me when she next went into town, but Mum said that wouldn't be necessary, she would be going herself in a couple of days.

As it transpired, neither of their services were needed. The following Thursday Mr Rodda from the tin stream works came and asked if I was still looking for work. He had friends with a small general store at Pool, a village about three miles away on the road to Redruth, and they were looking for a female assistant. He knew only that she had to be honest, able to read and write, add up money and be used to obeying orders. Added to this she would have to be able to deal with the customers in a kind and friendly way. He would be going home to lunch and would take me to see the shop owner on his way, and bring me back if I had finished my business when he returned.

I spent the morning getting ready. I made sure my shoes and clothes were as clean as they could be. I washed my hair, although it was unheard of to wash hair except on bath nights, but I had been out in the field working on the previous days and being fair-haired I wasn't sure it was as clean as it should be. I liked the sound of the work, the more I thought of it, I made up my mind I would not lose this job if I could help it.

Mr Rodda stopped the car outside our gateway, opened the car door and said "Get in Evelyn". I realised then how nice it was riding in a car as a proper passenger. I had been in trailers towed behind pick-up trucks working in the fields that were too far away to walk. Joan's dad's car, the only other one I'd been in, had been rather overcrowded.

I couldn't believe how quickly we arrived at the shop. Mr Rodda came in with me, to introduce me, he said. I felt important as I had never been introduced to anyone before. I took particular notice of how he did it.

The small shop had only one window and one door. Mr Rodda entered and I followed him down the one step and waited behind him. A grey-haired lady came from behind the counter, hand outstretched.

"Good afternoon Mr Rodda, I am pleased you were able to

get here" she said. (Except for close family people were not
called by their Christian names in those days, and even close
family were always addressed by their surname in front of young
persons.)

"Good afternoon Miss Powning, this is Evelyn Hugo, the
young lady I was telling you about" said Mr Rodda.

Miss Powning held out her hand to me. "Good afternoon
Evelyn, so you'd like to work in a shop would you?" she asked.
I wasn't sure what to say, so I just shook hands and nodded my
head. Mr Rodda stepped toward the door and opened it, saying,
"Perhaps you ladies will excuse me, I must get home for my
lunch". Miss Powning asked him, "Will you be calling in on
your way back to work or are you leaving Evelyn with us?"

He looked at me. "I'll call in, and if you're ready to go I'll take
you, if not then you can make your own way home I am sure."

I wasn't certain I could remember how we had got there, but
I didn't say anything. He left and Miss Powning locked the door
after him, saying, "He's quite right it is lunch time, and it is
Thursday so we are closed for the afternoon. Did you have your
lunch before you left home?"

I wasn't certain what she meant by lunch, as we had always
called food in the middle of the day 'dinner', but I said, "No, I
haven't had anything to eat since my breakfast".

The lady took hold of my hand saying, "Come and meet my
mother, then we'll go into the kitchen to find us some food."
She led me through a very short passage and into another room
where an elderly lady was sitting in a large high-backed chair.

She had a coloured blanket over her lap and lifted her head slowly to look at her daughter. She had beautiful snowy-white hair and a lovely soft pale pink skin. She was dressed in a pretty blue cardigan that matched her pale blue eyes, with underneath it a cream blouse with a lace collar.

"There you are, Mother, I've brought a young lady to meet you" said Miss Powning. She placed my hand to her mother's. The lady wasn't able to shake hands, so I just closed mine around hers and said good afternoon.

I instinctively knew this lady had been ill recently, as I had been taught how to deal with people who were not able to help themselves when learning first aid in my short time with the Red Cross. Though she could not acknowledge me, I liked this gentle lady and hoped I could spend more time in her company.

Miss Powning then took me to the back part of the property, where she toasted us some bread and poached a couple of eggs. While we ate she explained that a Mrs James would be calling in soon to prepare and cook lunch for her mother. Apparently her mother had had a stroke and could no longer care for herself. Before this she too had worked in the shop.

And so began what I hoped would be a long and enjoyable period of my working life. My new employers were Methodists; they knew of Roscroggan Church and were delighted that I was a regular member. Miss Powning was a member of the, Methodist Ladies' Choir at Camborne.

Apart from how to run the shop and care for the customers, there was much to learn about housekeeping for a small family.

I enjoyed everything about working there. Quiet periods were spent weighing up goods that were delivered loose, such as potatoes and other vegetables. Butter, cooking fat, dried fruit, cheese and dried fish were regular products that had to be weighed in small quantities.

The only item I found distasteful to handle, because it too had to be weighed, was plug tobacco. It arrived in an airtight tin to keep the tobacco moist. Square or round, dark brown in colour on the outside and half an inch thick, it was all coiled around on itself, like a miniature coil of rope. A length of it had to be pulled from the tin, cut off with a knife and weighed in half or one ounce portions. Occasionally this was asked for as 'chewing tobacco'. Another product much like it was twist tobacco. This too was sold in half or one ounce portions. I remember also the feel of the waxy paper it was wrapped in.

On the shelves too were cigarettes – Star, Woodbines, Park Drive, Kensitas, Players' Navy Cut and Craven-A, plus other brands of fine tobacco such as Wills Gold Flake, Erinmore and some which could be rubbed down between the fingers for making cigarettes by hand - 'rolling your own' as it was termed.

The shop next door was a Post Office, run by a Mrs Maddern and family. There was a son in the Army, and when he was home on leave he would sit in the back garden with a gramophone and play sentimental records such as ballads by Bing Crosby, Dennis Lotis and Dickie Valentine. How I loved listening to those songs. If I could arrange to be out in the back of our premises, weighing up goods, I would.

To our left was a butcher's shop, Pooley and Son, and beyond them was another small general store similar to ours. I believe the difference was that we also sold clothes. Across the road was a newsagents and confectioners. Pool also had a bakers, hairdressers, a fish-and-chip shop and a doctor's surgery.

Mrs James, the lady who came to tend Mrs Powning, lived directly opposite, which was very useful whenever Miss Powning had to go out of town on business, which I learned she often did on Thursday afternoons.

A surprise awaited me when I reached home that day. Mrs Mankee and family were leaving Roscroggan, having purchased a house at Roskear. It was a couple of weeks before they left, and although Mrs Mankee came to say goodbye I was at work, so an invitation was left for me to visit them whenever I was in the vicinity of their new home. I managed to call in when shopping at Tuckingmill on one occasion, but somehow the friendliness was missing. I never went again.

# CHAPTER 14

One day on my way home a small black open-top sports car pulled up beside me. It was the son of the fish and chip shop owner where I'd previously worked. He had left Basset Road Boys' School at the same time as I had left the girls' school. He claimed the car had been a 14th birthday present. Apparently as long as he had a licence, he could drive. There were no driving tests then.

He asked if I had got another job, and when I said yes and I was quite happy thank you, he informed me he could get me a job back in his mother's shop if I wanted. He said they had employed two other girls since I'd left. They too had not lasted. When I replied that it was probably due to the fish-man, he said I was too sensitive. I should have stood up for myself. When he realised I did not want to change my job again, he drove off.

I recall thinking that I hoped nobody had seen me talking to him, and reported it to Mum. Apart from the fact that he was a male, I would have to explain who he was. As the wages he offered were a little more than I was getting from Miss Powning, I might have been made to change jobs again. I decided to keep that knowledge to myself unless questioned at home.

Once a month the clothing coupons collected for goods sold at the shop had to be delivered and registered at a bank in Redruth. I remember the pride I felt when I was entrusted with this errand for the first time. It also meant travelling on a bus too, a real treat!

I had never done any business with a bank before, so I was apprehensive on my first visit. The young lady who dealt with me was very kind, and explained each stage as she went through everything I had given her. When she'd finished I felt I knew nearly as much about our registration as she did, and I looked forward to the next month.

Now that my job seemed to be established, Dad and the boys gathered together the necessary parts to construct a bicycle for me. In less than a week, becoming overconfident and hurtling pass the Tolvaddon Stacks, I struck a large stone and sailed over the handlebars. Result – badly damaged bicycle and knees, and the end of cycling for me.

We were now coming up to Christmas. This was the most important time of the year at home, as there was much baking to be done, and most of us were busy making presents and seeking hiding places for those already made and wrapped. I don't remember fancy wrapping paper, such as we have these days. Dad was very secretive at this time too, but the result was always worth all the secrecy.

On Christmas Eve decorations would go up, and this year Frances had been given a box of lovely coloured Chinese lanterns, a Father Christmas going down an imitation brick chimney to hang on the holly tree we always had, and some other pretty decorations. Added to the paper chains we'd made up ourselves, the house was going to look even better than usual.

The decorations had come from the mother of Butcher Williams, a lovely elderly lady who made a fuss of our pretty sister. She also gave her a selection of black and white pictures of soldiers drawn on parchment. I don't recall seeing those, but Frances says that to a child's eye they were very good.

Frances was lucky, or unlucky, in that her birthday was on Christmas Eve. She always had more presents to open than anyone else, and when we were opening ours on the day Frances had a pile she had opened the day before. She always had a special birthday cake made from the remains of the Christmas cake Dad had made. None of us begrudged her day; we knew our turn would come and she would have to wait a full year before hers came around again.

On Christmas Day, presents were opened first thing in the morning. On the bottom of our bed we were left a stocking or similar containing small gifts, an apple, some sweets such as liquorice allsorts or dolly mixtures, and maybe a pencil, a rubber and an exercise book. With the war on, several of these things were missing, so Dad often tried to make us small things like pencil cases or shoe bags for our school daps. The boys got woodworking tools.

Once the main meal was over and washing up done, out would come the table games, Ludo, Snakes and Ladders, Tiddlywinks and card games. Dad often made a giant cracker that was hung on the wall and filled with small gifts, each with a string attached. When one of us won a game we went over to the cracker, pulled one of the strings and out would come a gift.

Of course, occasionally the gift would be quite unsuitable for a child – a card of buttons, a tape measure or maybe a small tool – then we would exchange it with someone or give it to Mum or at times even back to Dad for next year's cracker. Christmas was always a happy time. I think the youngest children made it so, as they were always so excited that nobody wanted to spoil things for them.

For a couple of weeks nobody had to spend much time in the fields, which meant we could keep the table games going. Now that I was working of course I had to go back after the festive holiday, which for me was only two days. Frank had taken over my paper round after school, although I still had to do it on Thursdays on my half day from the shop.

In six weeks I would be fifteen, and three days later Frank would be fourteen. Mum was already talking about Frank leaving the grammar school, saying she still needed more money coming in. I was surprised that Dad didn't object, but he explained to Frank that at his age he had already been working down the tin mine for two years because he was unable to get an apprenticeship, which was all he wanted for his sons, so that they would have a secure future.

Frederick was at this time only twelve, so he did what he could to help out in the fields, but he was already showing signs of looking after himself with buying and selling at school items such as comics and marbles. Later came chicken, other jobs not necessarily connected with the fields and more adult salesmanship. He had more courage than the rest of us and no qualms about bartering with people. He seemed to do well, though nobody else knew how much money he actually had for his efforts. He always gave Mum some of his earnings. I don't know how he got away with it, as I was told to hand over all I'd earned and Mum would give me what she thought I should have.

I had once been asked to sell daffodils for three brothers, retired men by the name of Cattheral, to whom I delivered papers at South Tehidy. They had large grounds with orchards and suggested I should get what I could for the spring flowers but hoped I might get 4d a bunch. When one man only gave me 2d I couldn't argue, and just accepted it. Frederick, I'm sure, would have done better.

I got into trouble over that on one occasion too. Apparently someone had seen me handing over the cash I'd got from selling the flowers to one of the brothers, who always came to their gate to save me walking down the drive to the house a second time. The accusation that I was accepting money from men was the result. A denial and the request that she check with the gentlemen concerned brought no help. Mum did not believe a word I said.

One Thursday late in the afternoon Dad and me went over to Tuckingmill. He had to see someone about a job, while I had shopping to do for Mum. I noticed that Dad's trilby hat had been scorched in the front. It was his practice to hang hats on a hook in the ceiling over the oil lamp to dry. I couldn't let him go for an interview in it, so I told him. He snatched it off, looked at it and flung it away. He thanked me and said he couldn't go out in it again. He did get the job in spite of having no hat.

A week later I was sent to Camborne for potatoes. I was passing the Co-op Gent's outfitters and saw a new trilby on a model in the window. The price was four shillings and eleven pence. All the way home I puzzled over how I could raise the money to buy that hat for Dad.

# CHAPTER 15

Frances and David were now the family representatives in the fields. They were working for hours, in spite of only being eight and ten years old. In fact Frances was at one time left in a field weeding until nine o'clock at night. Apparently she had been forgotten, and as she normally trotted off home on her own if the men were busy, no-one knew she was still out there!

Frances did love the job of weeding and working with the land. She enjoyed picking peas and potatoes and planting cabbages and so on, and of course she felt she was helping the family finances. As she was getting older she was learning. She noticed we had few cups, so we often used small jam jars to drink from. We had one glass tumbler, so the young ones fell out over who would get to drink out of that.

Bedding too was in short supply. When it was really cold coats became our extra bedding. Of course rationing was still very much with us, so even if we had had a lot of money to buy everything we were short of, certain items would still have been difficult to get hold of.

Frances was in a much better position than I had been when

I first arrived at Roscroggan, in that she had both boy and girl friends of her own age to play with. She also had the chance to visit them in their homes, so she was able to compare. The outdoor life has always been a preference for her as with David, and she admits to having been a bit of a tomboy growing up.

One day in May 1945 I was delivering papers to a house at Halgoss, near Tehidy, when the lady owner came rushing out with a glass of lemonade and a home-made bun. "This is for you," she said, offering it to me. "It's all over, the war is over, isn't that wonderful news?" I agreed and thanked her for the refreshments, but I didn't really appreciate what it would mean at the time.

Actually it made little difference to our way of life or what we could obtain in the shops as yet. That didn't stop street parties being held in Camborne though. I didn't think Mum really wanted to, but after all of us badgering her she finally agreed we could go up to Camborne to take part in what was going on as long as we all stayed together.

There was some singing and dancing, but we didn't take part in it. The boys cleared off somewhere, but we girls had to stay with Mum. There appeared to be thousands of people in the streets that evening. Two old schoolfriends passed and asked if I would like to tag along with them. Mum was standing there, and as expected she said I was needed to keep an eye on the younger ones.

Later at home the boys said they had met three girls who lived not far from us. One was Kathleen Kelly from Tuckingmill, one was Ashgan Turk from the top of the hill, and the other was Barbara Bennetts from Tehidy. All three were part of the group of six selected for the County School. They would have been schoolmates had I been allowed to go. When the boys mentioned they'd asked for me and suggested I might like to call and see them some time, Mum told the boys not to bother telling me as there was no way I would have time to be going anywhere with them.

I remember spending most of the time standing somewhere near Park Road, as everywhere else was too crowded for Mum to take the pushchair with the youngest children hanging on to the handles. Dad must have been working, for I don't recall him being with us. I don't remember any form of souvenirs on sale; I don't think there was any sort of official celebration until the following year.

Frances wasn't entirely happy at Roskear School. She thought her first teacher was extremely old because she wore very dark clothes and was stern looking. Apparently she would walk quietly up and down between the aisles of seated pupils and suddenly Frances would receive a hard rap on the knuckles with a cane and be told "Write with your right hand! She never could, and still doesn't.

Frances and Margaret recall that another highlight for them was the Sunday school 'tea treats'. Held on a Saturday when I was working, they claim they were all given a paper bag with cakes in and instead of sweets they had fresh garden peas which they were allowed to shell and eat on the spot. They'd then have races and prior to going home an extra large saffron bun. This is a traditional outing for Cornish Sunday schools and still continues for several of them to this day, although a visit to a seaside town by bus often takes the place of the local field.

Of course the boys and I had missed out on tea treats, as with the war on they weren't held regularly, although I do remember one occasion when I was given a tea treat bun out in a field. I suppose folk at the Sunday school couldn't look after so many children in case of air raids.

Another tradition in Cornwall is the Whitsun celebrations. A swings-and-roundabout fair arrives in Redruth prior to Whitsun week and stays at the Fairfield meadow at the top of the west end. It opens in time for the weekend, so a fun time is usually had by all.

On Whit Sunday hundreds of people gather at Gwennap Pit, where a religious ceremony is held in Memory of John Wesley, who preached there in the 1700s and described it as 'the most magnificent spectacle to be seen this side of Heaven'.

At that time it was simply an extremely large pit, hollowed out among the mine workings. Now it comprises many complete circles of what appear to be steps but are in fact used as seats, terraced since John Wesley's time as a memorial to this great man. It has been written that in the region of thirty thousand people listened to this seventy-year old preacher.

Dad took my two brothers and me on a visit to the fair one Whit Saturday. We had to walk of course, about an eight-mile round trip, but because of the treats, toffee apples, popcorn and a bag of chips at one stage, we considered it worth it. We also called on some friends of Dad's (name of Thomas) in Redruth, who gave us tea and buns.

On the Sunday we set out again from Roscroggan with pasties, saffron buns and home-made lemonade for a picnic on our way to Gwennap Pit. This was when we heard of John Wesley. I reported this excursion to Mrs Basset the next time we met. She was very pleased to hear about what I'd learned at the Pit. I chose not to make too much of the Saturday trip as I thought she might not approve of the fairground.

Occasionally on Fridays Miss Powning would ask me to stay at the shop for lunch. I would be sent to purchase fish and chips for us and having eaten, Miss Powning would sing to her mother and me. My favourite song was 'All in the April Evening' although I always found it difficult to show how much I enjoyed it. I was embarrassed at someone singing to me in such a confined space. Her mother loved it though.

I was really established in the shop now and customers would come in and ask where I was if they didn't see me immediately. Which made what happened one Sunday at Roscroggan even more frightful to me.

Frank and I were late for Sunday school. I suppose we had chores to do before leaving home that had taken us longer. When we arrived outside the building Mr Ashton was already addressing the other children, so we decided to wait until he had finished speaking before going in. Two boy friends from up near Roskear arrived on their bicycles. They stopped to ask what we were doing hanging around outside. When we explained, they suggested that it was time we had given up going to Sunday School anyway. They were a couple of years older than me and no longer attended. They then tempted us into going for a ride with them, promising to get us back for when the Sunday school youngsters came out.

We liked the sound of that and after walking up the hill we each climbed on to the crossbar of a bicycle and set off. Frank and his friend were much faster than Robert and me, so they were well ahead when we reached the top of the stretch of road where we turned left for Portreath. As we arrived there, so did a police constable, the local policeman for Pool and surrounding villages, coming from another road on his bicycle. He alighted, propping his machine against the nearest hedge and his hand went up, the flat of it facing us in a stop gesture. We stopped, and he pointed to the ground at his feet.

"Do you realise you are breaking the law?" he said.

I shook my head but Robert said, "No sir". I was trembling now, wondering what was to happen next. He pulled his notebook out of his pocket.

"Well I shall have to take your names and addresses, so come on Missy out with it please, what is your name?"

I couldn't speak. Robert stepped forward "Do you have to sir?" he said. "It's not her fault, I encouraged her."

"I'm afraid so my boy, the young lady is also guilty of breaking the law so her crime is as great as yours, so come along miss, your name is?"

"E-velyn—H-hugo," I stammered it out,

"And the address?" I knew he was looking down at me, willing me to answer, but I couldn't look at him.

"Number 2, Tehidy Mill Cottages, Roscroggan" I mumbled.

"That is good" he said. "I know where those cottages are, left just down the hill from the church aren't they?"

"Oh please don't tell my parents!" I was near to tears, really frightened now he knew where I lived. He stepped past me and repeated the request for his details to Robert. Now it occurred to me where he was stationed, Pool! That's where I worked! What if he came into the shop? What if he mentioned it to Miss Powning? I should probably get the sack. I'm sure she wouldn't want someone working for her who had committed a crime.

"Thank you, young man, now take my advice and get off home. No more riding two on your bike, you've no excuse now, you know the law don't you?"

Robert didn't appear too concerned as he said "Yes sir of course I do, what happens next?"

"You will be hearing from me. After I've reported to my superior officer he might want you to call at the station for a talk on what he's planning to do about it."

We set off, walking back the way we had come and not speaking until we were well around the bend and out of the policeman's sight. Robert touched my arm, saying "Your brother and his mate were lucky weren't they? I wonder where they got to?"

I couldn't answer - I was too close to crying. He stopped, coming around his bicycle and put his arm across my shoulder, pulling me closer to him. "Oh dear, you are upset aren't you?" he said. "Look I'm sorry, I should never have brought you on this road."

Of course that was enough to set me off crying, "I'm afraid! What do you think he will do about it?"

"There's not much he can do, I've never been in trouble before. I don't think they treat it very seriously if it's a first offence."

I shook my head. "I've never even spoken to a policeman before. I'm afraid of what will happen if he goes to see my parents."

"If you're over sixteen he won't do that."

"But I'm not over sixteen." I couldn't stop the tears.

"Well look, if there's anything I can do come and see me I'll speak to your dad if it's necessary."

Suddenly I became conscious of time going on. "What time do you think it is?" I asked.

As he was wearing his Sunday best, he had a pocket watch. He pulled it out of his pocket. "Twenty past three, not too bad, we'll be back at the church in ten minutes."

We hurried on, no thoughts of riding again. As he'd said, we were soon at the church. Standing outside waiting for us were Frank and his friend.

"Where have you two been? We thought you'd get here first" Frank asked.

"Pool copper stopped us" Robert replied. "You two did all right, got so far ahead he didn't spot you."

"Well thank goodness he didn't, what happened?"

"He took our names and addresses and says he'll be in touch. But for now Frank you will have to look after your sister, she's had a fright."

Frank looked at me, "Well for a start you'd better clean up your face. If Mum sees you've been crying you'll be for the third degree." He glanced around. "Go behind the church to the tap, the cold water will do the trick. Go now before the others come out, then they won't know we haven't been here all afternoon."

So it transpired. Nobody noticed anything and we all trooped home, but it wasn't until I went to bed that night that I could think about it again. Sleep didn't come easily. At work next day I dreaded every ring of the shop bell. If Miss Powning noticed anything, she didn't mention it.

As the week went on it got harder and harder to act normally. I had difficulty eating and sleeping and showing an interest in the younger children's activities. Even walking to and from work was laborious. Whereas before the incident I would notice every new leaf or flower, I couldn't think about my surroundings at all. I also dreaded meeting either of the two cycling friends, in case I should be seen talking to them. I was convinced there was someone watching me around the clock.

On Friday night I prayed hard that PC Furze would not make me wait over the weekend before getting in touch. At the same time I didn't want him coming to the shop or my home to contact me. I hoped he might be waiting to catch me on the way home from work, so when the shop bell went late on

Saturday afternoon I was shocked when Miss Powning greeted him!

"Good afternoon Constable, what can I do for you?"

"Good afternoon, Miss Powning." He touched his helmet, not removing it. "It's your young assistant here I'd like to speak to if I may."

Shaking like a jelly, I gripped the counter. He was watching me closely. He must have noticed the change of expression; there was no way I could have spoken to either of them.

"As long as you are not taking her away from us constable, you are welcome to speak to her. I couldn't do without her help, now you know".

"I am pleased to hear you say that, Miss Powning. Hard-working youngsters are so necessary these days with so many families losing theirs through them going into the services, But I'm not here to remove her from your premises. I'm hoping she can assure me regarding a little matter I've been investigating."

Miss Powning indicated the passageway out of the back of the shop. "Come along then Evelyn, take the constable in to the stock room, you can be private there"

He followed me out. I'm sure he could see me trembling. He appeared even larger and more threatening in this confined space and with his helmet on. I dreaded what I was to hear. He closed the dividing door, to stand in front of me.

"Well Evelyn, how has it been this past week? Been riding on any more crossbars?" He was looking at me sternly.

I was as frightened as I had been last Sunday. I managed a

"N-no," and a shake of my head.

"That I'm pleased to hear." He indicated I should sit down on one of the two chairs, though he didn't sit himself. "I have some good news for you" he said. I looked up; he was still watching me. "You remember I said I would have to speak to my superiors?" I nodded my head. "Well I did so, emphasising that it was your first offence, that you came from a good family, had a steady job and I would be keeping my eyes open for any more misdemeanours from now on." He hesitated, and I glanced up at him,

"I couldn't do any more, could I?" he went on.

He was waiting for an answer, but I could say nothing. I shook my head. He took out the notebook I'd seen before.

"I've made a note of the main points." He paused. "They're of the opinion that you were encouraged in this escapade by a person older than yourself, that providing you stay away from said person you are unlikely to make the same mistake again." He paused while he read his notes. "On my recommendation they are overlooking the crime this time, but mind what I say. Don't ever do such a thing again. Next time you won't get away with it."

It was some time before what PC Furze had said sunk in. He allowed me a minute before he spoke.

"So you do realise what this means don't you? You won't have to visit the police station or face my superiors, are you pleased about that?"

I stood up, but all the shakes hadn't gone. I managed to stammer, "Th-thank you sir."

He opened the door, saying "Shall we tell Miss Powning she won't be losing her assistant at this time?"

Miss Powning was straightening goods on the shelf behind the counter. She looked around as we entered. "Evelyn has been able to help you, has she constable?"

"Very much so, Miss Powning" he answered. "I will be able to close that particular case now, thanks to this young lady here."

"I am pleased to hear it constable, I knew she'd help if she could."

As usual I had to wait until Frank and I were alone that evening before I was able to put him in the picture. His reaction was much like my own, "Thank goodness that's over!"

# CHAPTER 16

Life became more settled for a while. A couple of weeks later a very nice Air Force blue coat came into stock at the shop. It was lovely, and Miss Powning encouraged me to try it on. It fitted me perfectly, and she wanted me to have it. It was priced at 12/6 (62p). I said I did not expect Mum would agree to my having that amount of money to spend as it wouldn't be fair on the other children not having the same spent on them. That was Mum's stock reply whenever I asked for money.

Later in the day Miss Powning worked out that if I paid so much a week, which she would take out of my wages, perhaps it would be all right. I waited until Dad was at home before asking about it. He said, "Bring the coat home and I'll think about it". When he saw it he said, "Yes" at once. Mum didn't agree, as she said the colour wasn't practical and it would get dirty quickly.

Dad suggested that after I had paid for the coat I should buy shoes in the same colour and by the same method. Miss Powning agreed, and very kindly got a lady friend of hers to make me a hat to match, made up of felt petals the same colour as the coat.

That, she said, was a late birthday present. When friends at Sunday school and church saw me they all said how smart I looked. I was careful what I said at home about it though so as not to be accused of showing off.

Unfortunately, Mum decided to take advantage of Miss Powning's generosity over paying for my things and started giving me lists of groceries each week that I then had to pay for out of my wages on Saturdays. This reached such an amount that some weeks I had no wages to pick up and a couple of times there wasn't even enough to pay for the groceries.

One week Miss Powning got a bit concerned and wrote a note to Mum saying she was not legally permitted to employ someone, especially a young person, and not pay them a wage in their hand each Saturday. Could Mum come to a more suitable arrangement about payment for the groceries, such as sending the money in for them. Mum refused to answer the note saying it was no business of anyone what she spent her money on and I was to tell Miss Powning so. Dad had no knowledge of these transactions, as obviously he would not have agreed. I had been told at the outset not to mention it to him.

It was a great temptation though, especially as Mum made no attempt to alter the situation, and every week I had to face Miss Powning with yet another list with no money to pay for the items on it, and have no wages to collect. This in turn meant I got no pocket money. I queried this. Mum said it was my contribution to the house, and everybody who went out to work was expected to pay for their food.

Frank, by this time, had got himself a job in engineering, in a foundry at the rear of the Holmans works in Camborne. I don't think he liked it and to make matters worse, he couldn't get an apprenticeship, which was the objective from Dad's point of view and the sole reason for him leaving school.

Frank and I couldn't understand the need for it. We knew that Family Allowances had started to be paid to mothers in the autumn of 1946. As it was to be 5/- (25p) per week, for each child except the first, which was me, it seemed strange that Frank had to give up his grammar school education just when more money was coming into the house and Mum was getting it paid to her.

It didn't help me either. Later too, new Acts of Parliament paid more and for children up to the age of eighteen if apprenticed or still in full time education, for which Frank would have qualified if he had still been at school.

One day Frank and I met Robert, the boy whose bicycle I'd ridden on, and he asked me if I would like to go to the pictures with him sometime. Of course I said I would not be allowed to. He found that funny, so Frank explained that Mum would never permit it. Robert said he'd heard about Mum, but what about Dad? Surely he was the head of the house? He also said his sister was allowed to go out if she wanted as long as her parents knew where she would be and who she was with in case they needed to get in touch. Somehow we managed to persuade him things were different in our house. But I liked the idea.

Some days later I found a blister on the heel of my left foot.

It was quite sore, so I put some St James's Balm on it, but it didn't go down. Within a few days it had turned a nasty blue colour and was a third of the size of an egg, Mum said it was nothing, it would soon break and I was to go on as usual, but Miss Powning was shocked when she saw it. She said I should be wearing stockings (something I was not permitted to do on account of my not being old enough) as it was probably caused by the dye of my shoe. She gave me sixpence to go home and visit the doctor.

I walked home, limping. Mum was cross and said I was fussing over nothing. I set off to Camborne, and got to the doctor's just before one o'clock. He said I should have come to him before the blister had become septic. Now he would have to lance it, and that would hurt. It did hurt, and no wonder with what came out when he cut it. He instructed me on looking after the wound, then got the surgery nurse to come and dress it.

After putting a special dressing to draw out any poison left in the wound she put a bandage over the whole thing and told me not to walk on it for a few days until the swelling had gone down. I didn't know how I was to get home without walking, so I didn't tell her where I lived. She then told me to keep the sixpence Miss Powning had given me to pay the doctor and buy myself a treat.

I had saved 1s 6d (7.5p) tips earned from flower selling and paper deliveries on Thursdays. This was in the pocket of my new coat at home in the wardrobe, and I planned on putting the sixpence with it towards the hat for Dad. I found it extremely painful with my shoe pressing on the wound, so when I got to the seat situated outside Camborne on a grass area at the end of King Street I sat down to rest. I'd been there about ten minutes when a Jeep pulled up and Terry, the eldest son of Captain Kelly, got out of it. I didn't know him very well. He had been working abroad for some years. He said to me, "You're one of the Hugo girls aren't you?" I said I was and he asked what I'd done to my foot. I explained. He said he had intended coming to the cottage to ask if some of us children would come to the farm to help with picking sprouts, and now he offered to give me a lift home so I could tell my brothers and sisters what he needed. I was so relieved that I didn't have to walk any further on my sore foot.

On reaching home he helped me out and drove off. Mum wanted to know whose car I'd come home in. I told her and gave her Terry's message. She said the lift wasn't necessary as my foot wasn't that bad. I told her what the nurse at the surgery had said about resting, but she said I still had jobs to do, as housework didn't get done on its own.

Somehow I did manage all my usual chores by hopping around on one foot, except for fetching water. No way could I cope with that. To add to my trouble I was bitterly disappointed to find that the money I had left in my coat pocket had gone. It was all I could do not to scream 'Thief!' at everybody. I told myself it was my own fault for being deceitful in hiding it in the first place, and I would have to think of something else in future.

Dad said I had better not try walking to work on the foot for a few days – in fact he insisted I stay at home until I'd seen the doctor again, which I did a week later. The doctor seemed to know I had not rested as instructed; he said that if I had done so the swelling should have gone down much more than it had.

He gave me another dressing to put on after the present one was exhausted and again said to stay off the foot as long as I could, and no school for another week.

I didn't trouble to correct him about my working instead of school. It would make no difference at home – I would have to do the best I could. I was still limping when I returned to work the following week. Miss Powning wasn't happy with my returning to the shop so soon, but I managed to persuade her that the walk to and fro caused me more pain than being there in the quiet of the shop. She gave me easy work to do, such as sitting by the till and taking the cash. She also suggested I stay to lunch each day until I was back to normal.

# CHAPTER 17

It was a couple of weeks before I could return to going home at midday. Before that happened Miss Powning suggested I went to Camborne Wesley with her one evening a week and join the same choir as her. It would mean staying for tea with her and going on to Camborne by bus afterwards.

I didn't think this would be permitted at home, as I would be getting out of my usual chores, but Dad said I was old enough now to do something grown up of an evening and I would be in church, so it was all right. The choir were practising the Hallelujah Chorus, by Handel. I found it very difficult to sing, as it was much too high for me, so after a few weeks I had to give up.

Being allowed to go out of an evening gave me hope that I might be permitted to go somewhere else, such as the cinema. So when Robert knocked on the cottage door one Sunday while we were at tea and asked to speak to Dad, I half hoped for success. He asked for permission to take me walking on either Sunday afternoons or after Church in the evenings. Dad asked him for a few personal details and then told him I was too young to be going out with boys and for him to come and ask again when I was sixteen. I think Dad might have forgotten I would be sixteen on my next birthday, only months away.

Dad had bought a 'His Master's Voice' gramophone, and with it he'd been given some twelve-inch black vinyl records with a dark red label in the centre depicting the HMV white dog sitting next to a large trumpet-like instrument. Around the label was printed 'His Masters Voice'. There were records by Paul Robeson, Joseph Locke and Peter Dawson. He'd also received a small square tin of needles, today called 'styluses', which were slightly thicker than a sewing needle and about three quarters of an inch long. They had to be placed in a slot in the end of the arm. When the arm was directed over the groove of the records the pointed end of the needle rested in and traced the groove around the record until it reached the centre, enabling the music to be heard.

Female singers I remember were Gracie Fields, Shirley Temple and popular stars from the music hall such as Marie Lloyd. Another was of Dame Clara Butt, whom I learned from Miss Powning had been awarded her title during the war for her work for charity. She had a beautiful voice. On this record she was singing 'Softly Awakes My Heart' on one side, but I can't remember what was on the other side. My favourite though, was 'The Volunteer Organist' by Peter Dawson. Years later I was able to purchase a set of coloured postcards with that song in words and pictures on them. I still have them, and it's as much a favourite today as it was then.

During the war years places of entertainment such as theatres, cinemas, dance halls and anywhere crowds would gather, even football matches, were closed down. It was stated that if such places were hit by a bomb large numbers of people would be killed or injured unnecessarily. People were also encouraged not to gather together, for the same reason.

The new year, 1947, brought bitterly cold weather. With only one pair of shoes I had to be careful not to get them wet. When it came to walking to work in the snow I walked in bare feet and carried my shoes. At least they stayed dry for working all day. (I might add here that I have never suffered from chilblains.)

I met Robert on the way to or from work occasionally. He worked for a builder, who lived and ran his business not far from our cottage. Robert would be the first to arrive at the builder's yard in the mornings. There were no lorries for small businesses in those days. Robert would harness the horse, get the cart loaded with whatever was required for the day's work and set off ahead of his boss to the day's location. Whenever they were working in our locality and we met, he would ask me out or offer me a lift on the cart, and I continually refused. It became a joke as we both looked forward to my being sixteen.

Robert was quite a musician. He sang well, whistled tunefully and played the harmonica with skill. Often on a summer evening when I was fetching water I could hear him playing across the valley. I was getting romantic feelings about him, and found myself hopeful of seeing him each time I set out from home.

Frank and Frederick pulled my leg about him, but were very

careful not to mention it near the cottage. I was also aware that some of our neighbours knew I wasn't allowed to go out by myself or have girlfriends, and although I never talked about it I somehow got the feeling that the neighbours would all agree with Mum and think I should do more at home.

It was about this time Frederick recalls Mum flying into a temper and throwing a dish of cereals on to the floor. She shouted about being pregnant again. The following evening she was outside in the garden talking to Mrs Mankee. I had just finished helping the young ones into bed, but as I went down the path to fetch water, Mrs Mankee said "Hello Evelyn, how are you?"

I was surprised. nobody had ever asked me that before.

"I'm all right, thank you," I said.

"I'm glad I've seen you," she said, " Jean wants to go to Roskear to the pictures one day next week. Would you like to go with her? I'll pay for you both of course."

Before I could think of what to say Mum answered. "She's not old enough to be going out in the evenings on her own and I don't agree with girls wandering the streets at night."

"Who said anything about wandering the streets? It's only at Roskear." Mrs Mankee laughed. "There's a cartoon film on that Jean wants to see."

Mum had already started to make her way indoors, and she turned to me and said, "Get on with what you're doing and don't hang about, I'm waiting for that water".

"You're making a rod for your own back, Frances," Mrs

Mankee called to Mum. "You can't keep your kids with you for ever and they'll never grow up if you don't let them."

"Mind your own business!" Mum said and went indoors. I carried on to the water chute. I thought about what had happened and felt sad. Now mum had given Jean something else to laugh at me for.

I had got the two buckets filled and was almost back to our path when I heard someone whisper my name. "Evelyn!"

I put the buckets down and looked around. The voice came again, "Evelyn, I'm here behind my hedge in the garden." I realised it was Mrs Mankee. I could just spot her coloured apron through the hedge. I wasn't quite in sight of our front room window, so I whispered back to her.

"Yes, I can see you."

"I'm sorry if I've caused any bother for you Evelyn. I hoped that by mentioning it with mother there it would save you asking and she'd say it was OK."

" Oh, that's all right Mrs Mankee, I'm used to it." I picked up my buckets and went indoors.

With the water deposited safely, Mum said "About time too, I suppose that nosey neighbour came to fetch water as well?"

"No, she didn't." I said.

"You hadn't better be lying, my girl. You stay away from her and her ideas, and stay away from her girls. They're too old for you."

Of course it was more than I dared do to correct her and say that Jean was younger than me. Before removing my apron, I asked what else there was for me to do. For once there was nothing, and I was told to go to bed. I had very unhappy thoughts that night.

The following Thursday after the paper round I had to go shopping with Mum. While she was in the Co-Op grocery and I was looking after the pram outside, two of my old schoolmates came along. They asked where I worked and seemed pleased to know I had got a job. Because they hadn't seen me in town before they assumed I was working on the land. We had no time for more, as Mum came out of the Co-Op and called me. I got a bit of questioning as to who the girls were and what they wanted, and she hoped I hadn't been planning on sneaking off with them some time.

Dad was to be made redundant, a new word in our house. The Purcel family he worked for had made a bad investment on the stock market and were going out of business if they didn't cut down on staff. For a few days he went from farm to farm asking for work. Lots of them were in the same boat; the money they were getting for their produce was barely enough to feed their stock and with the bad weather they were unable to put cattle out to graze.

There was no fieldwork to be had either, so life at home was hard for everyone. Dad still had a few sewing jobs, but the odd few pence he received didn't go far. I talked to him about asking a bit more for his work, but he said he might not get any work at all if he did so as other people were having difficulties too.

I wondered if he regretted not accepting the job he had been offered by the Singer Sewing Machine Company. This was when we had lived at Penryn, before the war had made everything so difficult. Apparently someone had shown a Singer representative a sample of Dad's needlework and an agent had called on him offering to set him up in a premises where he could run a little business using their machines and doing all the repairs and alterations that came through their business. He told me that as he and Mum already had four children at that time the pay would not have been enough.

He was due to attend the Labour Exchange the following Friday, and hoped they might have something to offer him. Meanwhile he said he was sorry, but there'd be no birthday party this year. I wasn't too concerned, as I had other things on my mind. I would soon be sixteen, and Robert was to come and ask to take me out again.

# CHAPTER 18

The weather continued to rule everyone's lives The snow that had fallen for weeks through January and February had frozen solid. People who were wealthy enough to own their own transport were no better off, as they were unable to drive. The horse and cart came into good use again delivering the goods, as it had before the advent of the motor car, and small vans were becoming popular.

Dad got a temporary job at the gasworks at Tuckingmill, taking the place of someone who was off with an injury. The big thaw came in March, and I recall reading of floods in some parts up country. I suppose it was due to the snow melting and swelling the rivers.

I had managed to go to work every day in spite of the weather. Nobody extra was wanted on the farm. The cows had been kept in the barn most of the time, so Freddy Butler had looked after them himself. The milk was always ready after 4 pm, so no delays there. The boys and I were no longer expected to milk the cows or collect eggs.

At last the day came when grass began to show through the

thinning white snow. Our lives started to get back to normal. On the first Sunday when the roads were totally clear of snow, Robert knocked on our door. I was sixteen years and two months. I couldn't hear what was said, but it couldn't have been much before Dad shut the door. My mother asked who it was. Dad said "That boy again."

He looked at me. "You may as well know, he asked to take you out. I told him no."

"But you said when I was sixteen..." My throat was choked up. I couldn't get any more words out.

"I know what I said but I didn't say you could go out with him, I only suggested he called again."

I knew that everyone was looking at me. I stood up pushing my chair back. "Sit down," my mother said, "other people are still eating."

Tears were running down my cheeks now. I hated being made to cry. "And you can stop that noise" she laughed. "Oh, he should see you now, see how grown up you are." At that moment I thought my parents were the cruellest people in the world.

The meal was finished in silence. The remainder of the evening followed as normal, except that nobody spoke to me. I imagine they didn't know how to speak to the big sister they'd never seen in tears before. Sister Frances squeezed my hand as she climbed into bed, which nearly started me crying again. At ten years of age, perhaps she was wondering what I'd done.

One week Lena Rule met Mum in town. In spite of the fact

that Mum didn't like Lena, she did speak to her occasionally. Lena suggested I might like to go and spend an evening with her and the children and later Mum told Dad, who asked why she would do that. She'd told him Lena had said she had a plant which I'd admired. This was true, it was a Busy Lizzie (Impatiens) which in the summer she kept on a table in her porch; I saw it each day as I left her newspaper beside it. We often talked about it. Apparently she planned on re-potting it and giving me a piece to grow on for myself.

Mum said "I told her Evelyn wouldn't know anything about indoor plants so she best give it to someone else and there was no reason for her to invite our children in to sit in her home, thank you."

Then came the day Mum was taken poorly. I had already gone to work. Freddie Butler apparently drove her into Redruth Hospital, where they decided she should stay until the baby was born. Dad expected her home again in a day or two. Meanwhile I was to stay off work until she returned in case anything happened.

I walked in to work next day to tell Miss Powning. Few people had private telephones then.

Dad's temporary job at the gasworks had come to an end, and he started the normal trek to the Labour Exchange each day but there was nothing. Then came a new ruling from the Government. All men on the dole and drawing money each week had, in the future, to accept jobs away from their own area if offered. Dad was exempt from the scheme because of his large family, but he asked to be considered.

A couple of weeks later, when Mum was still in the hospital, I had an accident with a saucepan of boiling water, spilling it over my foot. A huge blister appeared. Dad popped it when he came home and plastered it with St. James' Balm. I put a clean sock on it and walked about with no shoe on.

The following day Dad went into the hospital, insisting Mum came home as he couldn't cope without me and Mum. The nurse told him the baby wasn't due for another few weeks, so Mum was to take care what she was doing.

Mum wasn't very happy with me once she was home and realised I wasn't as useful as I should be. Dad was a great help, but of course it meant that while he was at home all day he wasn't earning wages.

I went back to work as soon as I could put a shoe on. The pain gradually eased and by the time Mum had to go into hospital again I was back to normal. This time Mum had another boy, Michael, the fifth boy and the ninth child.

Lena Rule was married to a stepbrother of Uncle Percy, Aunt Evelyn's husband. She always claimed a relationship with us, but Mum denied it. Lena's husband Freddy worked for Holman Brothers; as such he earned good wages and they had a very prettily turned-out cottage quite close to where Robert's boss had his home and business. They had two school-age children.

Freddy was an excellent singer. He was a member of the very popular Holman-Climax Male Voice Choir. It was difficult to become a member, so everyone guarded their places jealously. Practices were well attended as a result and Freddy never missed going.

During the next few weeks all of us had to do what we could to earn extra money to make up what Dad got for dole money. Mum barely spoke to me, and in turn I didn't feel like saying much to her either. Life was miserable, except for the hours spent away from the cottage.

I sneakily kept a few pennies back occasionally and when I was given tips by newspaper customers, I hid them in a handkerchief in the navy school knickers pocket I was still having to wear, as I was considered not old enough to have anything different. When I'd got enough to pay for a cinema seat at Roskear Picture House, I sent a message to Robert to meet me afterwards on the road home.

Frank and I fetched the water that evening and once we reached the front gate I put the buckets down and ran, not telling him where I was going. No one I knew worked at Roskear Cinema, so I was safe from tale-tellers.

Robert and I met after the film and stood in a gateway near Williams the Butchers from where I could see the cottage path, in case someone should be sent to look for me. I told him how miserable my life was. He said his mother had heard something from someone and wondered if I had talked to anyone outside the family about going into lodgings until we had saved enough to decide what our future together could be. We discussed the possibility of my doing that, but living where I did and working all day, I had little time to find out who I should get in touch with. It was a big step for me, so he said he'd speak to his mum again and maybe she would help by finding out some of the details for me.

At that moment we heard footsteps. Dad appeared out of the gloom. We had not noticed the cottage door open.

"Is that you Evelyn?"

I replied. "Yes Dad."

"Don't you think it's time you were home? Your mother is wondering where you've got to, it's gone ten o'clock."

"I'm on my way now, Dad." I touched Robert's hand, "I'll see you again."

My Dad asked, "What was that you said Evelyn?" I repeated it. He said to Robert, "I thought I told you not to come hanging around again?"

"Robert looked at me, "Surely Evelyn is old enough to decide for herself who her friends are. I've tried to do the right thing and ask your permission but for some reason you have decided to forbid it, so if we have to meet on the quiet then so be it."

My father chose to ignore that and started to walk off down the lane. I followed him, leaving Robert to gather his bike. A few minutes later he passed us, saying, "Goodnight Evelyn".

As we walked my father said "Do you realise how angry you have made your mother? It's lucky for you that I'm home."

I was nearly in tears. "Mum is always angry with me anyway," I said. "Nothing I do pleases her. I go to work every day, I do everything I'm told to do at home and I work in the fields in the evenings and weekends and I still don't get any pocket money."

Dad made nothing of that, except to say, "That's a housekeeping matter. You must speak to your mother about that."

We had arrived at the cottage. Dad went in first.

"Where was she?" My mother asked.

"Up by the Butchers', talking to that boy."

"I knew he'd be behind it, she deserves a good hiding after you telling him to stay away."

I walked in the room to hang my coat in the wardrobe.

She pulled me round to face her "What do you think you're playing at staying out till this time of night? And you went off without telling me where you were going."

I couldn't answer, and when she realised I was saying nothing she slapped my face and pushed me away, "Don't ever do that again. Now get to bed."

Thinking I'd got off lightly, I went.

The next morning at breakfast Dad told me he was going up to see Robert's parents in the evening. If all went well he would have a serious talk with the boy's father and maybe if I behaved myself we could meet up occasionally. I couldn't wait for my working day to be over.

I should have known that all had not gone well when Dad returned after only being gone for half an hour and threw his cap on to a chair with a "Well that's that".

"Oh" said my mother, "What's he been up to?"

"Huh," Dad said. "The father is the bloke who came and took that gasworks job away from me."

"You mean he's the man who'd had the accident, then claimed the job back?"

"That's right," Dad said. "Not only that, but he is a

Conscientious Objector." (I had no idea what that was.) "He did nothing to help in the war and while people like us struggle to earn a living he's lording it over everyone with a smart home and three of them working full time, wanting for nothing."

"So what did they have to say?" my mother asked.

"Say?" said my Father, "He laughed! That ignorant man laughed, he said him and his wife never interfered with their kids growing up. It was better to let them make their own decisions and their own mistakes."

"How old is that boy?" My mother asked.

"That one who came here is nineteen, the other is twenty-one. Well I warned him there'd be trouble if their nineteen-year-old didn't stay away from me and mine. Ignorant people! they were still laughing when I walked out! Call themselves Christians! Huh!"

I couldn't understand Dad talking about Christians, as he and Mum never went to church except for one or two of our own children's christenings, whereas Robert's family did regularly.

"You heard what your father said, my girl," my mother threatened. "Stay away from that boy! If I catch you anywhere near him you'll get what you deserve."

For a couple of weeks everything carried on as normal. Then Dad got a letter asking him to go for a medical examination prior to reporting to the Labour Exchange for an interview for the up-country job. He passed the medical and two weeks later 80 Cornish men, including Dad, were shipped up to Chippenham in Wiltshire.

The Firm was The Westinghouse Brake and Signal Company. They manufactured engineering products, such as couplings for railway trains and rectifier fins for aeroplanes.

# CHAPTER 19

***

The men were housed in a hostel. Such was their dislike of the job, given the long hours spent away from the family with no possibility of a trip home for some while to come, that a few months later only two men, Dad and a Mr Tresidder from West Cornwall, remained in Wiltshire. Some, mostly tin miners, had gone further up country to the midlands to get work in coal mines, but most had returned to Cornwall.

Life was much the same at home. There were more products appearing in the shops, such as Hugo's Tinned Preserves, (I always like to imagine these were manufactured by relatives of mine, although they came from abroad according to the label), but there was never enough money to buy anything new.

One Thursday when I delivered Lena's paper she gave me a half a crown, instructing me to hide it in my shoe and tell Mum I was going to the pictures with her. She said she didn't want Freddy to know she was paying for me and he often checked her purse to make sure she had enough money. I smiled to myself after leaving her – of course I never *told* my mother anything, I *asked*.

Much to my surprise my mother made very little fuss about my going out, so I set off early after tea to Lena's cottage. Freddy answered the door, and when I asked for Lena, he told me she was upstairs with the children, and offered to give her a message. I said we were going to the pictures and should I wait for her or walk on ahead.

Another surprise awaited me. I must have made a mistake, he said, it was his choir practice night, and Lena couldn't go out because he wouldn't be there to look after the children.

I heard someone coming down the stairs and Lena appeared. Behind Freddy's back she was signalling something that I took to be 'go on ahead.' She said "I'm sorry, I'll see you soon". I stopped outside their gate, wondering what to do. I still wasn't sure Lena would be coming, but maybe she'd got someone else to look after the children that Freddy didn't know about.

Meanwhile I had the money, and if she caught me up later she would need it, so I couldn't go home. I was in two minds. I could imagine the trouble I'd be in if Mum found out I'd gone on my own, but I was out on my own now. I would be seventeen next birthday. Why not do what I wanted for a change?

I constantly stopped to glance behind me. No one was coming after me, not even Lena. I reached the Scala before I realised Lena had not told me which picture house she'd intended going to. Mrs Warne's daughter Dorothy was the cashier in the box office, so I asked her to tell Lena I'd gone in if she turned up. I paid 1s 3d (6p) for second best seats, as I didn't want to be down the front. I think the Film was 'Love Story'. I can't recall who was in it, but I think Patricia Roc and Stewart Grainger were among the cast.

Many different emotions passed through me as I sat there. Of course I should have gone back home. I had not been given permission to be out on my own. Had I done so, one of the boys might have been allowed to come with me.

Then I thought about the money. I might have been forced to hand that over and still not allowed to go to the pictures. I knew though that I was in for trouble if someone saw me and got to Mum before I reached home.

I glanced around in the interval, but saw no sign of Lena. I decided that if she had come maybe she would see me. But the film ended and she didn't show up, so I made my way down the stairs to leave through the Skating Rink Exit. I was on the stairs when someone touched me from behind. I turned and there was Robert.

There were lots of people surrounding me and I was at the bottom of the stairs before we could speak. "I thought you weren't allowed out on your own?" he smiled.

"I'm not" I said, "I'm supposed to be with Lena Rule, but she hasn't turned up."

"Well, I'll walk you home if that's all right, but I've got to go to the back to pick up my bike, I've been skating."

We stopped by the door and that was when I heard "Evelyn!" My mother's voice! I turned, and she hauled me off the step and gave me the usual slap across the face. Robert turned back, as did a few other people.

"There's no need for that Mrs Hugo, Evelyn hasn't been with..." That was as far as he got.

"You keep your mouth shut and stay away or you'll get some, as big as you are." She waved her hand in front of his face.

It was then I noticed my brother, Frederick. He had been standing behind out of the way. He came closer and mouthed something at me. I pushed my way past my mother and ran. I had no idea where I was going, but of course instinct took me down Fore Street, past King Street and on to the Tehidy road. My mother was shouting, but I ignored her. I was still picturing all those people outside the Scala staring. I thought I should never show my face in Camborne again.

Somehow I stumbled, walked and ran, with Frederick and my mother chasing after me all the two miles home. Frank must have been left in charge, as he was the only one about when I nearly fell into the cottage door. I had just about got my breath back after taking time hanging my coat in the wardrobe when my mother shouted from the kitchen.

"Come out here!" She was waiting with a stick. I got it across my shoulders and back. I had no defence, and whichever way I turned she turned, lashing out with the stick and shouting at me all the time. I have no idea what she said, but I heard Frederick's voice begging her to stop.

With a final shove and a "get to bed!" it stopped. I slept very little that night. I was in pain and trying to plan my future away from her. I'd never before disliked anyone as strongly as this woman who, without asking questions, could beat her daughter in such a wild way. Every instinct said 'run away', but how could I run away, with no money and nowhere to go? I couldn't even get on a bus. I could not ask Miss Powning, as I was sure she would not approve of my leaving home at my age.

Next day I discovered the 'stick' used on me had been the cane removed from the net curtain that had hung over the kitchen door glass.

It was many years before Frederick told me what had happened that night. Apparently after I had been gone from home for an hour Mum had sent him over to Lena's house with a women's magazine. I've often wondered why she suddenly felt the urge to do that, as she wasn't even friendly with Lena. When he returned he had been questioned as to who had opened the door to him. Some time later he had been told to get his coat on and come up to town with her to look for me, and had been sent into the cinema to ask Dorothy if I was inside. So my mother had then waited outside, stewing on my wrongdoings, and I had walked right into the trap. Frederick had apparently begged her to stop beating me or she would kill me, and he too had then been threatened, but it had stopped her.

I don't know whether she ever found out the truth from Lena or even tried to, as it wouldn't have taken much effort. I never spoke to Lena again. I put the remaining one shilling and three pence (I'd have replaced the whole half crown if I'd had pocket money) in a used envelope I'd begged from Miss Powning, and dropped it through her letterbox with her newspaper, so I'm sure she knew how I felt about her.

The outcome was that whenever Mum went out anywhere the boys were to make sure I never went outside the house. I was instructed to do all the indoor chores and the boys were to do all that was needed outside. I wasn't to answer the door. If anyone was to come calling the caller was to be asked to come back when Mum was there to speak to them. I had no respect for my mother, and bravely suggested she ought to tie me to the table leg to make sure I didn't escape.

I never told Miss Powning about that incident, so when a letter arrived from Dad telling Mum to prepare for us all to move up to Wiltshire, I found it difficult to explain how I felt about going. Miss Powning wanted me to remain in Cornwall, and was quite prepared to have me live with her. She offered to pay me a small wage and all my keep. Needless to say Mum would not permit it.

I didn't know at the time, but Dad had asked Mum to send him the Roscroggan rent book. It was needed for a reference enabling Dad to rent a property from the council at Corsham, a small town near Chippenham, which people working for Westinghouse were permitted to apply for provided they had no bad debts against them. Frederick said Mum was in tears over that, because she was behind with the rent and expected our move would be off. Apparently when the rent book was not forthcoming Dad, always enterprising, produced his own version. It was accepted by the authorities and we were allocated a bungalow in Corsham. In truth we were allocated two bungalows which had been knocked into one especially for a large family.

I learned that Frederick too had been offered a home with the people he worked for if he'd like to stay with them. He couldn't accept either.

A few days before we left Cornwall, Frank asked Frederick to go with him to a now closed tinworks to collect scrap metal, some of which was brass. Frank loaded it in a sack and on to his bike and sold it to the scrapyard where he worked. Most of the proceeds went to Mum, some to pay for refreshments on the forthcoming journey. She also borrowed what money Frederick had left to do the shopping when she got to Corsham. He never did get it back. As he said, "Par for the course".

It is evening, July 1948. We are standing as a family group on Camborne Railway Station. Ahead of us lie who knows what changes to our lives? Behind us, an empty cottage. We carry with us the memories of seven years living in the hamlet of Roscroggan.

And so we caught the overnight passenger train to Corsham in Wiltshire... but that's another story.

The end

# FOOTNOTE

Camborne in the 1940s

In Trelowarren Street, Camborne's main street, were Liptons and Pearks (grocery stores) and Timothy White's, which sold soaps and pet foods such as dog biscuits, and some items people would use in the kitchen. There was also W H Smith for stationery, newspapers and good-quality reading matter like the books I could only read in school.

In some of the side streets were small shops selling home-made sweets, toffee apples, cakes and pastries. Quite often these were no more than the front rooms of the terrace cottages Camborne mainly consisted of. There were shoe repair shops with small home-made leather goods for sale and places where we could take the accumulator from our radio to be recharged. I usually paid four pennies for this, but I didn't know what was done to it. I was always told to be very careful not to drop or damage the accumulator. I believe it contained acid.

There was also a large greengrocer's by the name of M J Tellam. Opposite the town clock was Tyack's, a well-known hotel. Next door was a large draper's and ladies' clothes shop by the name of Rice's, one of many drapers' shops dotted about the town. Tyack's also boasted an ironmonger's, with a bicycle shop next door. I used a lane behind Tyack's, between it and the School of Mines, on my way to school.

Hanging over a wall on one side of the lane were some fruit trees; one at least was a medlar tree. I had never heard of this fruit before. When I was given one to try I thought it was already over ripe and didn't care for it. I was to learn many years later it is the only fruit that is eaten when decayed.

There was a Cornish Laundry somewhere behind the wall; I remember the smell and steam rising but had no idea where it was sited.

There were at least four hotels with public houses. I remember going to Aunt Evelyn's on an errand for Mum and cousin Lizzie telling me her Dad was home on leave from the Navy and her mum had gone up to town to have a drink with him in a pub. I had never heard of a woman doing such a thing before. My own parents never did, I'm sure.

A few yards from the town clock was the Parish Church. There was also the Methodist Church in Wesley Street and the Centenary Chapel close to the Holman Works, which had been built as an overflow to the Wesley when Methodism was prolific in Cornwall. The Salvation Army was a popular place of worship. St John's Roman Catholic Church stood in Trevu Road, near the railway station. At Tuckingmill was All Saints Church, another large building. A smaller United Methodist Church stood at North Parade, Roskear. In the centre of Trelowarren Street was another United Methodist Church.

There were several other churches and chapels in the surrounding villages. As we never attended any but our own at Roscroggan, we knew very little about them. A few steps down the hill from the railway station, several roads join. The area is known as The Cross (the cross it was named for, which originally stood nearby, was removed to the grounds of Trevu House in the mid 19th century). Here stands the public library. I was informed that the original building for housing books had been known as the Literary Institute and sited in an old cottage in Wellington Road.

In 1894 J Passmore Edwards, a well-known philanthropist, laid the foundation stone, and the following year he officially opened the free library where it now stands. Money for the books and equipment was bequeathed by one Octavius Ferris, from Highgate in London. It is said that the books were worth £2000, the same amount as the building had cost. He had done the same for other libraries in Cornwall. The books from the Literary Institute were also donated. Local folk who were interested in improving their knowledge made full use of the books, and the library flourished.

On 17th May 1932 Prince George unveiled a statue of the great engineer Richard Trevithick, the area's most famous son. He stands proudly in front of the library, holding a model of one of his inventions, the steam engine known as 'The Puffing Devil'.

The largest employer of the area was Holman Brothers, manufacturers of mining machinery and equipment since 1801. I learned later that the railings and gates that had once enclosed the Roscroggan Methodist Church had been manufactured and supplied by the Holman Works. The firm was known and their products sold worldwide. Although at the start of the war scores of men had been called up for the services and many others volunteered, Holmans still had many hundreds of men in and out of their gates each day. A number of bomb shelters had to be built to protect their staff.

In 1942 Holmans manufactured components for tanks, Bailey bridges and aircraft landing gear. Holman's rock drills and compression units were used in training personnel from the Royal Engineers. In 1943 it became necessary to employ women to work on some of the extra units that had to be built to cater for Government orders. Women were being conscripted at that time. Camborne was also surrounded by mines, once producing copper, now mainly supplying tin, and employing hundreds of men.

In that same year King George and Queen Elizabeth visited the Holman's works. Much of the talk in Camborne days after they'd gone was about where they'd walked and the number of people who saw them 'near as I'm seeing you, out of my window as they passed my house'. A never-to-be-forgotten visit, considering there was a war on.

Frances grumbled about the visit because they had to go to school and stand outside by the railings waving flags until the important visitors had gone. The children were then given their morning allocation of a third of a pint of milk and sent home. A long walk for nothing, according to Frances.

ND - #0442 - 270225 - C14 - 203/127/14 - PB - 9781861512260 - Matt Lamination